MW00977221

Auditing Markets, Products, and Marketing Plans

AMA MARKETING TOOLBOX

David Parmerlee

NTC Business Books

NTC/Contemporary Publishing Group

Library of Congress Cataloging-in-Publication Data

Parmerlee, David.
      Auditing markets, products, and marketing plans / David Parmerlee.
            p.   cm. — (American Marketing Association marketing toolbox)
      ISBN 0-658-00133-7
      1. Marketing audits.   I. Title.   II. Series.
      HF5415.16 .P37   2000
      658.8′02—dc21   99-56227

This book is dedicated to those I left behind.

Cover design by Nick Panos
Cover illustration copyright © Rob Colvin for Artville
Interior design by City Desktop Productions, Inc.

Published by NTC Business Books (in conjunction with the American Marketing Association)
A division of NTC/Contemporary Publishing Group, Inc.
4255 West Touhy Avenue, Lincolnwood (Chicago), Illinois 60712-1975 U.S.A.
Copyright © 2000 by NTC/Contemporary Publishing Group, Inc.
Printed in the United States of America
International Standard Book Number: 0-658-00133-7
00   01   02   03   04   05   VP   15   14   13   12   11   10   9   8   7   6   5   4   3   2   1

Contents

Preface

Many marketing management books only define marketing and provide terminology definitions. The AMA Marketing Toolbox has a different purpose. This series will guide you in analyzing and articulating marketing data and applying it to real-world marketing actions. Definitions are included to form the basis for effective marketing management. The narrative aspects of these books describe the components of marketing processes. These books define the relationships between the processes and explain how they all work together. They also supply sample formats to help you create sophisticated marketing documents from your data.

A Systematic Process

Because markets change constantly and new marketing techniques appear all the time, a step-by-step system is needed to ensure accuracy. The books are process-based to allow you to be as thorough as possible in your marketing activities and document preparation. The books address marketing for the consumer package product, business-to-business, industrial manufacturing, and service worlds.

For Marketers

Although these books are written with a how-to theme, they are written for experienced marketers who know marketing terminology and understand the business function of marketing. The AMA Marketing Toolbox series consists of three books:

- *Auditing Markets, Products, and Marketing Plans*
- *Developing Successful Marketing Strategies*
- *Preparing the Marketing Plan*

Role of the Marketing Management Audit

How does the marketing management audit you will perform fit in with the other marketing processes? The marketing management audit is the first step in this series. It identifies the market in which you are or will be marketing your products, defines the products you are or will be marketing, and evaluates the effectiveness of the marketing actions you are or will be employing. It determines what, why, how, when, and where events and activities have or will be happening. This marketing tool helps you assess your strategic direction and how you will program your annual marketing plan actions.

The books in the AMA Marketing Toolbox series will help you evaluate the markets and the customers you serve, the products you offer, and methods in which those products are marketed. The following diagram indicates where the books fit into this process.

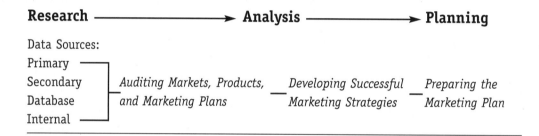

Research ⎯⎯⎯⎯⎯→ **Analysis** ⎯⎯⎯⎯⎯→ **Planning**

Data Sources:
Primary
Secondary   *Auditing Markets, Products,*   *Developing Successful*   *Preparing the*
Database   *and Marketing Plans*   *Marketing Strategies*   *Marketing Plan*
Internal

Introduction

What Is Marketing Management?

When one poses this question to various business executives, their replies are almost always broad or abstract. To underscore the various interpretations of this subject, ask ten business executives to describe how marketing as a business function contributes to their company's success and you will probably receive ten different answers.

This situation exists because marketing suffers from an identity crisis like no other business function. Accounting, manufacturing, or human resources, for example, all are considered to be fairly well defined; marketing, on the other hand, is not. The reasons for this situation are so numerous it would take another book to explain them. Instead, this book addresses this facet of marketing management by defining the established standards.

To produce and implement a pure balanced marketing plan, marketing management must be practiced by the organization or customers it serves. As businesses struggle to define what marketing is, they also need to devote their energies to defining how it should be organized around customers and products. Changes in technology, a diverse global economy, and sophisticated customers who are media savvy and demand more value are dictating that marketing management be a complete and strong aspect of a company's business practices. The marketing plan must reflect not only the plan for action in a given year, but also an approach to marketing that is not just a glorified sales plan or media-buying strategy. To survive and succeed in today's marketing landscape, companies must move from "power and control" to "empowerment and cooperation" of marketing individuals. New methods such as sales automation, integrated marketing, process-based marketing, or digital media access must be employed.

Marketing management is the *management of the process of developing marketing thoughts*. It is the ability to isolate, control, and program the function and functions of marketing. If it were not for the function of marketing, the capitalistic or free enterprise system would not exist as we know it. Thus, marketing is the activity that bridges the item of value for sale with the customer who wants or needs that item.

How Does the Audit Process Fit into Marketing Management?

It takes preparation to produce a marketing planning document (strategic or tactical) and to administer the actions and results profiled in that document. In the world of marketing, preparation translates into gaining accurate and timely data to make wise decisions.

A marketing audit, like an accounting audit, is an instrument to measure the value, risks, and effectiveness of your marketing efforts. Although it is considered to be a separate animal from traditional primary and secondary research, it augments those data collection efforts by focusing internally on recorded performances and on past and present views of the future.

How Often Should a Marketing Audit Be Performed?

The frequency and the degree of detail needed to generate the appropriate marketing information will vary. Some companies will perform a complete audit every year. Others will conduct an audit every four years, with modified versions used in between. Depending on the complexity of a given industry and the amount of growth or change it is experiencing, the timing of a marketing audit will differ. The key is to perform a complete audit (to form a solid baseline) in establishing your marketing approach, and then update that information as you feel it is warranted.

The Marketing Management Audit

How Does a Marketing Management Audit Work?

A marketing management audit consists of reviewing three fundamental elements:

- how you view and approach the markets you serve
- the value of the products you offer
- the effectiveness of the actions used to market those products

These three elements form the basis of a marketing management audit and the overall structure of this book. The following sections in the Introduction will explain how you can use the marketing audit to uncover the information you will need to shape your eventual marketing activities.

The Market Audit Element

A market audit is an attempt to define the structure of the environment in which a company operates—the marketplace. Its function is to collect information and organize it in a fashion that alerts you to marketing needs, problems, and opportunities. This information becomes a document that provides a detailed, accurate, and unbiased view of the marketplace.

Why Perform a Market Audit?

The purpose of performing a market audit is to find out what to expect from the marketplace you are currently in or are considering entering. It provides you with data on any barriers or limitations you might encounter in entering or expanding into a market so that you can determine what it will cost to exist or compete. It also tells you what the possible return will be; in other words, what the market is worth to you (market value) or what you can expect in terms of revenue generation (sales volume/earning potential). The market audit is the base from which you will develop strategies and tactics to achieve these returns.

A market audit builds the foundation for future marketing decisions. The golden rule in performing a market audit is that you must be objective and read the market as it actually is. This means the audit must not be structured around your product, service, or business. Though these may be mentioned as reference points, don't make them central to the audit. To do so could result in conclusions slanted toward your business, giving you an inaccurate picture of the market and defeating the purpose of the exercise. The audit is based on market research activities and must be completely independent from research on the performance of your product, service, or business.

The Product Audit Element

A product audit is an attempt to isolate and assess the worth of a particular thing you sell to generate income. Its function is to collect and analyze data in an accurate and unbiased manner to determine the value of your products to your company.

The product audit gives you a clearer understanding of your product line dynamics in a set format. It establishes why your products exist, how they contribute to the success of your company, and their impact on the marketplace. A product audit has to answer the following questions:

- What needs do your products meet or what problems do they solve?

- How profitable are your products? Which are strong or weak?

- How many products can you produce now and in the future? Will that meet demand?

- What possible legal actions do you face when marketing your products?

- What new products are you or should you be introducing?

Why Perform a Product Audit?

Like the market audit, the product audit tries to be as objective as possible: to "read" your products' value or purpose as it actually is, with little or no interpretation. The audit should mention the markets targeted with these products or services only as reference points; to do otherwise could result in conclusions slanted toward your product or business, thus giving you an inaccurate picture of your product's well-being and defeating the purpose of the exercise.

Think of a product audit as a player evaluation used to select a team to compete in a sporting event. Like a baseball manager, you have certain capabilities—your product offerings—that you believe will allow you to compete and win where the game is played—in the marketplace.

The chicken or the egg question—which comes first—always applies when you are determining market impact versus product impact. In this example, we are assuming that you will define and identify your market by performing a market audit prior to the product audit. The environment where you want to compete exists; you are now trying to determine how to select and use the players, your products. To do this, you must assess your products individually and collectively to determine their strengths and weaknesses.

First evaluate your product capabilities—their features and benefits. Then determine where they are in their life cycles. How many good years do they have left? Concurrently, you need to examine each product's contribution to the "team's" efforts. Some contribute more than others; this can be good or bad depending on the individual product's role.

Next you need to evaluate each product's past and future sales performance. If you have a "rookie player"—a new product—then you must predict its level of performance based on current conditions. As you perform this exercise, try to identify slumps and sales fluctuations to establish patterns. Then calculate how profitable your products are. With each product, you have made an investment and, as with any financial risk, you are spending money in the hope of making more money.

The next step is to determine production capacity for each product, the "team's" ability, its resources, and your liability for each product.

Finally, you need to determine what new products will be coming on board through product acquisition and what products you have in the research and development pipeline. How will new products help your product line?

Like a pro baseball team, your product line is the way you win, through sales volume and revenues. To win the game, you must identify and cultivate "players" who can perform consistently and produce a solid return for your investment.

The Marketing Actions Element

A marketing actions audit is an attempt to evaluate the mechanism of the internal management of your marketing activities. Like its relatives, the market audit and the product audit, the marketing actions audit collects and analyzes data to arrive at results that are detailed, accurate, and unbiased.

The marketing actions audit gives you a clearer understanding of your marketing department in a set format. It assesses how effective you have been at setting and achieving sales, revenue, market share, and profitability goals. It examines your level of efficiency in marketing your products by the activities you have used, the cost of marketing, and the control procedures used in your marketing operations and organization.

As with the other two audits, you need to perform the marketing actions audit as objectively as possible, examining how your marketing operations are performed, with little or no interpretation. The audit should mention the market and products or services only as reference points; to do otherwise could result in conclusions slanted toward your marketing actions, thus giving you an inaccurate picture of your marketing management and defeating the purpose of the exercise. The market audit (where you will be marketing) and the product audit (what you will be marketing) should have already been completed. The marketing actions audit (how you will be marketing your products to the market) will link the market audit and the product audit together to give you a total picture of where you stand.

The Role of the Marketing Audit

The marketing audit tells a story about the marketing of your product offerings to the marketplace. It explains what, why, how, when, and where events and activities happen. The marketing audit tells you if your sales and revenue forecasting have been accurate and whether they have produced sufficient growth to cover your costs and generate suitable financial earnings. It also measures how you are approaching your marketing efforts. A marketing audit should be performed every three to five years on the average. If your products have a short life span (e.g., high-tech products) and you are constantly introducing and terminating products, you should probably perform a marketing audit each year. The marketing audit is the first section in a strategic marketing plan, which is performed every three to five years, compared with a marketing plan, which is performed every year. A marketing audit would not be appropriate for a new business; a business plan would be a better alternative.

Reporting the Findings

Once the audits have been completed, you will need to document your findings. In preparing your report for the next step (marketing analysis and planning), be sure to include the following elements:

- title page or cover page

- table of contents

- executive summary (purpose of the analysis and major findings)

- methodology

- limitations

- market analysis (body of report)

- exhibits

How Should This Book Be Used?

This book provides you with a set of audit formats to help you prepare a document that presents marketing research data in an organized manner. Throughout this book, you will be alerted to adjustments you may need to make in the audit. To conserve space, each format shows a limited number of lines for products, whereas your firm may have fewer or many more products to consider. Some formats call for sales of a product for the past three years, but if your product is new, you will have no sales to date, making the current market share analysis impossible.

The processes and formats in this book are designed for the consumer package product industry; however, when a specific issue requires a separate and clear definition, other industries (industrial manufacturing/business-to-business and service) will be profiled.

Exhibit 1 profiles how these three audits work together.

Exhibit 1

Audit Overview

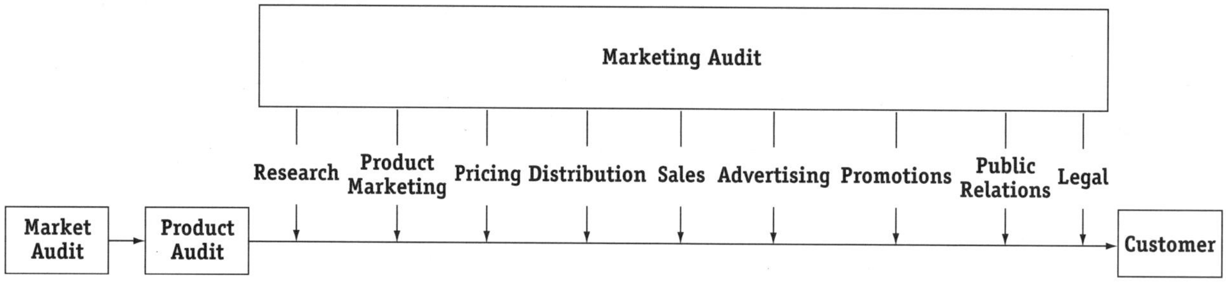

The marketing management audit begins with the market audit and is followed by the product and marketing audits. Follow the first three units in the book to reach completion.

Unit 1

Identifying the Primary Marketplace

The first step in conducting a marketing management audit is to review the market in which your business operates. To accomplish this, you need to dissect the elements that form the structure of a marketplace. This begins with the element known as *market definition*, which entails interpreting how you view the types of customers you are targeting. This effort establishes the foundation from which you will assess the resources and thought processes needed to market your products successfully.

Market Definition (by Industry Type)

In defining your markets, you are putting a face on the market as it exists today. This is the one place where you are afforded the opportunity to view the market in a subjective manner. This is because you need to decide on the size, complexity, and strength of a market you are willing and able to pursue. After this exercise, every element that goes into forming each one of these markets will need to be completed in a more objective manner.

You have two options to select from in defining a market:

- mass market

- markets divided into segments

Limiting yourself to selected market segments to gain more control in those segments is usually most effective. Market segmentation begins with marketing research. Before you can segment your market, you must understand customer preferences, motivations, purchase intentions, and usage patterns to establish linkages and verify the market profiles you select.

Depending on the industry you serve, market segmentation and variables that are used to define customer attributes (characteristics) drive how you will determine which customers are available. Although other variables should be considered, such as customer profitability, customer status (new, current, or former), and customer relationship (life cycle marketing), you may want to include these variables as part of your market segmentation/target marketing efforts.

If you serve the consumer package product (CPP) or service industries, Exhibit 1-1 illustrates the steps in selecting variables to define your market. In these markets, you will use geographic, demographic/socioeconomic, product usage, lifestyle/psychographic, synchrographics, shopping habits, and media usage variables. Service industries vary greatly, so you may need to modify this model.

Exhibit 1-1

Market Identification Model

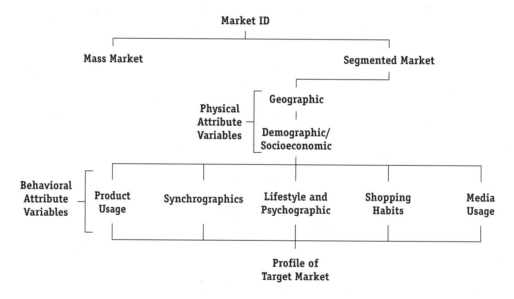

If you serve the industrial manufacturing or business-to-business (IMB) industry, Exhibit 1-2 illustrates the steps in selecting variables to define your market. In this market, you will use geographic, demographic, product usage, and media usage variables.

Exhibit 1-2

Market Identification Model

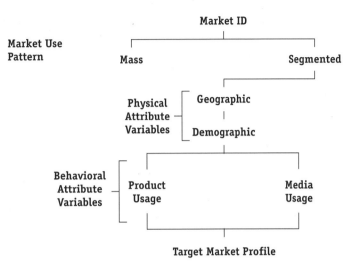

Target Market Profile

With both industry-specific models, you can select a type or combine several types of variables to form your market segment profiles.

Exhibit 1-3

Market Identification Process

1. Select market use patterns.
   a. Mass (If selected, skip to "Market Size Determination," page 19.)
   b. Segmented
2. Identify segment markets.
   a. Select variables.
   b. Establish profile segments.
3. Define target markets.
   a. Evaluate profile segments' attractiveness.
   b. Select/prioritize profile segments.

Once you select your markets, it is helpful to provide titles, or IDs, to each market you have targeted—for example, the U.S. home consumer electronics market. This will force you to truly define and establish (in terms of scope and purpose) the market or markets you will be committing your product and marketing resources to capture.

Market Segmentation and Your Target Markets

Identifying your market segments is called *target marketing*. The secret is to find a market where you can be a dominant player or at least a major player. To do this, you must establish criteria to penetrate and compete effectively in those target markets. The segmentation profile is made up of one or more physical or behavioral variables that must be prioritized.

You may need to go through the market segmentation process several times to determine which market definition works best for you. The key to the whole process is the geographic location(s) of your market. As discussed, you must perform market research before you begin the entire market audit process. That research will help you identify, define, and analyze potential customers for your product or for similar products in the selected market. The objective is to take that research data and match it with variables in the segmentation process so that you can see which geographic area has the highest number of potential customers.

Geographic Variables

You will almost always need to set physical boundaries for your market. This is done by selecting one geographic level or combining several, depending on your particular market. Geographic variables should be determined separately for each product line or individual product, if necessary.

To complete the table in Format 1, you must first select the level of the geographic area you choose to study. To give that level an identity, you need to call it by name (i.e., Census Tract 7301.03). You should identify not only the level you select, but several levels above it. This will give you a better point of reference and help you select the area(s) with which you wish to compare your target market. You will need to perform this audit for each product or product line you are considering.

In the CPP or service industry, all geographic levels are available for market definition. In the IMB industry, your geographic levels will be more limited because customers are fewer in number and cover a larger geographic area.

Format 1 displays the geographic levels available. They are based on the geographic levels established by the U.S. Bureau of the Census. Many research and database sources recognize these geographic levels as well as other "media-based" (e.g., ADI, zip codes, etc.) geographic levels. You may want to include these media-based levels as subgeographic levels so that you will have an equivalent basis of measurement when examining existing research data.

Demographic/Socioeconomic Variables

After you decide the physical area of your markets, you need to profile the possible customers in those areas. This is done by inserting the demographic/socioeconomic data (DSD) for those areas. With CPP and service industries, DSD

Format 1

Geographic Variables in Market Segmentation

Levels (Standard Unit)	Defined Area	
	Selection	Represents
Global/International		
National		U.S.
Regional		
Divisional		
State		Illinois
County		Cook
Minor Civil Division/ Census County Division (e.g., townships)		
Places (city and town)		Chicago
Census Tract/Block Numbering Area (population)	X	7301.03
Block Group		
Block		
Street		
Place of Residence/ Place of Business		

addresses human beings. With the IMB industry, you are focusing on demographic variables that address businesses. In the IMB world, you rely primarily on SIC (Standard Industry Classification) codes to define your customer type.

SIC codes have been used for many years to identify businesses, but the federal government is in the process of replacing the SIC code system with NAICS (North American Industry Classification System). This change is addressing the need for more modern and detailed identification of businesses. The basic framework is similar and provides the same type of information: defining a business type at the lowest level and presenting statistical information linked to individual business addresses and target market businesses. Government and commercial syndicated data vendors are the sources of business data and coding systems.

With the IMB industry, demographics tend to focus on size, industry behavior, and how a business operates (a business personality). The CPP and service industries use demographic along with socioeconomic data to define customer or household types by gender, age, martial status, education, occupation, ethnic origin, income, and housing patterns. In all industries, each company has its own database full of variables and attributes that will be helpful in segmenting the marketplace.

The key in market segmentation is to use it in a manner that allows you to see how customers exist, based on the similar characteristics found. In other words, you need to drop in the numbers of human elements that exist in those areas. Each format provided in this section of Unit 1 is designed to produce results based on the premise of that format. However, to really use market segmentation, you'll need to cross-tabulate each format. That means you take, for example, the geographic format and reference it to one or all other formats to show the number of customers who buy a product (product usage), in volume and frequency, by the various levels of geography. To accomplish this, you'll need to use a statistical or spreadsheet software package or the services and software of a syndicated data vendor to produce the ultimate market segmentation results.

The first two variables used to convert the geographic numbers into population numbers are demographics (the who) and socioeconomics (the what). These variables are based on U.S. Census Bureau counts of actual people and households, rather than on statistical extractions that may not accurately reflect the actual people and households in those areas. Census-based data is a more reliable indicator of the basic structure of the population occupying the area you are evaluating.

To complete Format 2-1, select the overall area or universe you wish to compare with the area you want to define. Remember, this is just an example—you may want to include other headings in your format such as degree of penetration (%). Drop in the numbers you have obtained from various sources in the columns for units, percentage, and index (which compares the two defined areas).

Index represents a formula that gives you a benchmark to determine how the two areas rank or rate. Interpretation may differ from vendor to vendor, and your understanding may differ from the source that prepared the data. However, indexing in this environment is generally performed according to the following formula (using the demographic/socioeconomic variables shown in the CPP industry):

Sex:

Male	
Overall area percentage	$\dfrac{42.67}{40.28}$
divided by	
Defined area	
multiplied by	$\times\ 100$

$$\frac{42.67}{40.28} = 1.06 \times 100 = 106$$

The number 100 gives you a baseline for comparison. If your defined market scores above 100, it has a higher propensity to accept your product. If it scores below 100, it has a below-average propensity to accept your product.

The table provided in Format 1 can be used for CPP, service, and IMB industries. For demographics and socioeconomic variables, the format tables will be different. Format 2-1 addresses the CPP and service industries, and Format 2-2 addresses the IMB industry.

The ranges provided in Format 2-2 are only examples. The ranges and the extent of the area you are segmenting may differ, based on your data needs and the source of your data. Format 2-2 provides an example that is typically available through syndicated data vendors. You can also perform this exercise using your own customer information from your database. You can expand your descriptors to include the following possibilities:

- types of customer service locations (e.g., rural, suburban, urban, etc.)

- sales performance patterns

- financial and operational risk

- key financial indicators (e.g., cost, sales, profitability, etc.)

- legal structure

- decision-maker identification

Product Usage Variables

After determining the physical area and the demographic data counts, you will establish the customer's behavioral attributes. Here you profile the various uses for a product or service and determine the various levels of purchasing activity, the factors that influence purchases, and the best methods of reaching those individuals regarding their purchasing decisions. To do this, you will select one or more product usage variables.

You can use the table in Format 3 for all industries. Like all the formats provided, you can customize your tables to reflect the market data you need or the information your data source provides.

In the CPP and service industries, many products offer similar features and benefits to a similar market type. The objective here is to evaluate a product with similar features to yours to determine how successful your product might be in that same market. Your goal is to measure consumption of similar products and to rate them based on volume. You will need to perform this audit separately for each product line or individual product under consideration. For example, if you sell toothpaste, you will want to compare your product with another that is similar in name, packaging (pump or tube), form (gel, paste, or powder), and flavor (mint or regular).

Format 2-1

Demographic/Socioeconomic Variables in Market Segmentation

Overall Area (Universe): *State/Illinois*

Defined Area (Target): *Census Tract/7301.03*

Descriptor	Defined Area		Overall Area		Index (%)
	Units	%	Units	%	
Sex					
Male	3,108	40.28	4,703,110	42.67	106.00
Female	4,637	59.72	6,320,197	57.33	96.00
	7,745	100.00	11,023,307	100.00	

Age distribution

2–5
6–11
12–15
(14–17)*
16–19
20–24
(18–24)*
25–34
35–44
45–49
(45–54)*
50–54
55–64
65–74
75 or older

*Note: variations in age breakdowns due to vendor variations.

Marital status

Married
Widowed
Divorced or separated
Single (never married)
Parent
Living together

Education (last grade attended)

Grade school or less (grades 1–8)
Some high school
Graduated high school
Some college (at least 1 year)
Graduated college
Graduate study
Full-time student
Part-time student

	Defined Area		Overall Area		
Descriptor	**Units**	**%**	**Units**	**%**	**Index (%)**

Format 2-1 *(continued)*

Demographic/Socioeconomic Variables in Market Segmentation

Occupation

Armed forces
Employed
    Full time (More than 35 hours/week)
    Part time (Less than 35 hours/week)
    Hold more than one job
Self-employed
Unemployed (looking for work)
Occupation
    Managerial
    Professional
    Technical
    Administrative support
    Sales
    Operative/Non-farm laborers
    Service workers
    Private household workers
    Farmers
    Craftsmen
    Other
Not employed
    Student (full time)
    Homemaker (not employed outside home)
    Disabled temporarily
    Retired

Ethnic classification

White
Black
Hispanic
Asian
American Indian
Other

continued

Format 2-1 *(continued)*

Demographic/Socioeconomic Variables in Market Segmentation

Descriptor	Defined Area		Overall Area		Index (%)
	Units	%	Units	%	
Annual household income					
Under $10,000					
$10,000–14,999					
15,000–19,999					
20,000–24,999					
25,000–29,999					
30,000–39,999					
40,000–49,999					
50,000–74,999					
75,000–99,999					
100,000+					
Household producers					
Full-time earner					
Part-time earner					
Dual earners					
Size of household					
(Age 18 or younger):					
None					
One					
Two					
Three or more					
(Over age 18):					
None					
One					
Two					
Three or more					
Householder status					
Rent					
Own					
Live with parents					
Type of housing unit					
House					
Apartment					
Condo/townhouse					
Mobile home					
Other					

Format 2-1 (continued)

Demographic/Socioeconomic Variables in Market Segmentation

Descriptor	Defined Area		Overall Area		Index (%)
	Units	%	Units	%	
Lived in area					
Less than 1 year					
1–2 years					
3–4 years					
5–10 years					
11 or more years					
Total					

Format 2-2

Demographic Variables in Market Segmentation
Industrial Manufacturing/Business-to-Business Industries

Overall Area (Universe): *State/Indiana*

Defined Area (Target): *Census Tract/4001.01*

Descriptor	Defined Area		Overall Area		Index (%)
	Units	%	Units	%	
SIC Code					
632302	26	100.00	334	100.00	
Annual Sales ($)					
$100,000–$499,999	8	30.77%	80	23.95%	77.84
$500,000–$999,999	6	23.08%	89	26.65%	115.47
$1,000,000–$1,499,999	5	19.23%	120	35.93%	186.83
$1,500,000–$1,999,999	6	23.08%	40	11.98%	51.90
$2,000,000–	1	3.85%	5	1.50%	38.92
	26	100.00%	334	100.00%	
Employees					
100–499	7	26.92%	90	26.95%	100.09
500–999	8	30.77%	79	23.65%	76.87
1,000–1,499	6	23.08%	110	32.93%	142.71
1,500–1,999	4	15.38%	50	14.97%	97.31
2,000–	1	3.85%	5	1.50%	38.92
	26	100.00%	334	100.00%	

Format 3

Product Usage Variables in Market Segmentation

Product Comparison Type: *Brand X*

Overall Area (Universe): *State/Illinois*

Defined Area (Target): *Census Tract/7301.03*

Descriptor	Defined Area		Overall Area		Index (%)
	Units	%	Units	%	
Heavy	1,002	12.94	3,034,872	27.53	213
Medium	3,020	38.99	5,866,101	53.22	136
Light	3,723	48.07	2,,122,334	19.95	42
Total	7,745	100.00	11,023,307	100.00	

In the IMB industry, the principles are the same, but there are the obvious differences in products. In the CPP and service worlds, a product or service is normally a finished item marketed to the end user (customer). In the IMB world, a product is a part or in support of a bigger product item. The customer is another business, not the end user. The product can be a customized part, so comparisons are sometimes difficult to make. As a result, product usage analysis may be used, but conditional assumptions must be cited in addressing all performance issues.

Lifestyle and Psychographic Variables

Another method of defining your market is through the use of lifestyle and psychographic variables. (See Formats 4 and 5.) This method, used in the CPP and service industries only, identifies and measures personal traits and behavior patterns. This information can aid you in forming customer profiles, but it is important to understand the limitations of the psychographic technique. It is very effective in defining markets for big-ticket items, such as luxury automobiles; it is not very effective in markets for low-cost items. When using psychographics in profile analysis, keep in mind that it should only be used in conjunction with other variables, and not as a single source for decision making. You will need to perform this audit for each product or product line you are considering.

Another variation of a lifestyle variable is something called *synchrographics*. It means looking at a customer's buying behavior from the standpoint of his or her life cycle—in other words, identifying events in one's life. This is also commonly referred to as customer life cycle marketing or customer relationship marketing. This lifestyle variable is used only for CPP and service industries. Events such as marriage, birth, relocation, new home, retirement, and more can all be applied in this market variable. No format has been dedicated to this vari-

Format 4				
Lifestyle Variables in Market Segmentation				
Overall Area (Universe): *State/Illinois*				
Defined Area (Target): *Census Tract/7301.03*				

	Defined Area		Overall Area		
Descriptor	**Units**	**%**	**Units**	**%**	**Index (%)**
Restaurant preferences					
Fast food	3,034	39.17	5,321,893	48.28	123.00
Full-service	2,332	30.11	4,389,100	39.82	132.00
Fine dining	2,379	30.72	1,312,314	11.90	39.00
	7,745	100.00	11,023,307	100.00	
Leisure-time activities					
Airline travel					
Sports participation					
Live entertainment					
Attend movies					
Rent videos					
Cable TV					
Home electronics					
Health care usage					
Hospital preference					
Clinic preference					
Insured					
HMO coverage					
Banking/financial affairs					
Investments (i.e., stocks)					
Debt financing					
Credit cards					
Debit cards					

continued

Format 4 (continued)

Lifestyle Variables in Market Segmentation

Descriptor	Defined Area		Overall Area		Index (%)
	Units	%	Units	%	
Auto ownership					
Lease					
Own					
Bought new					
Bought used					
Foreign					
Domestic					
Total					

Format 5

Psychographic Variables in Market Segmentation

Overall Area (Universe): *State/Illinois*

Defined Area (Target): *Census Tract/7301.03*

Descriptor (Group ID)	Defined Area		Overall Area		Index (%)
	Units	%	Units	%	
Upper crust	34	0.44	17,008	0.15	34.00
Lap of luxury	12	0.15	28.021	0.25	167.00
Established wealth	14	.18	11,073	0.11	61.00
Total	60	.77	57,102	.51	

able because of the uniqueness of each business's market and customer type. If this variable can be used in your environment, you can apply the headers in Format 4 to view the appropriate data.

Shopping Habits Variables

For CPP and service industries only, you can define your market by measuring shopping habits by customer, product line, and place of purchase. (See Format 6.) This enables you to identify where purchases occur in relationship to the

	Format 6				

Shopping Habits Variables in Market Segmentation

Overall Area (Universe): *State/Illinois*

Defined Area (Target): *Census Tract/7301.03*

Descriptor	Defined Area Units	%	Overall Area Units	%	Index (%)
Retail store preference					
Department store	1,045	13.49	2,023,755	18.36	136.00
Specialty store	2,334	30.14	5,658,898	51.34	170.00
Supermarket	1,298	16.76	1,000,230	9.07	54.00
Convenience store	2,674	39.61	2,340,424	21.23	54.00
	7,745	100.00	11,023,307	100.00	
Shopping motivation					
Price					
Selection					
Service					
Quality					
Location of store					
Purchase patterns					
Store					
Catalog/direct mail					
TV shopping					
Cash/check					
Credit card					
Coupon					
Brand label					

continued

	Format 6 (continued)					
Shopping Habits Variables in Market Segmentation						
	Defined Area		**Overall Area**			
Descriptor	Units	%	Units	%	**Index (%)**	
Major purchase intentions						
Car/truck						
Computer						
Furniture						
Appliances						
Home						
Leisure						
College education						
Electronics						
Total						

shopper's workplace and home. The objective here is to identify where customers shop and what influences their decisions to purchase. This information is very important when you get to the customer profile units where you will link customers by where they shop and where they live and work. This is called store-specific analysis. You will need to perform this analysis for every product or product line you are considering.

Although this variable is designed to be used in the CPP and service industries, the concept can be applied in IMB industries with a different approach. By looking at purchasing habits of a customer (another business), or by focusing on the purchasing agents or managers, you could apply this concept to build a predictive model. Although syndicated sources might provide this data, your own internal database can help you assemble the information.

Media Usage Variables

Another useful measure is the types of media customers use in discovering a product and forming a desire to buy it. The objective with this variable, seen in Format 7, is to establish what type of medium is used and when. If you are assessing the impact of television on behavior, you may wish to determine program viewing habits for even more detail. You will need to perform this analysis for each product or product line you are considering. Once again, depending on the vendor, some sources will combine these media activities and give you multiple usage data, while others will total each item and provide single source usage data to determine the media usage level.

Format 7

Media Usage Variables (by Medium Used)

Overall Area (Universe): *State/Illinois*

Defined Area (Target): *Census Tract/7301.03*

Descriptor	Defined Area		Overall Area		Index (%)
	Units	%	Units	%	
Direct					
Mail	803	10.37	1,256,450	11.40	110.00
Phone	75	0.37	999,767	9.07	935.00
Outdoor					
Billboard	345	4.45	2,311,189	20.97	471.00
Transit	176	2.27	1,998,900	18.13	799.00
Television					
Cable1	1198	15.47	4,783,991	43.40	281.00
Broadcast					
Radio					
Spot					
Print					
Newspaper					
Magazine					
Insert (FSI)					
Special					
Yellow Pages					
Total	7745	100.00	11,023,307	100.00	

The media analysis format can be used for all industries with some minor modification for the IMB industry. You will need to know if your data indicates time usage: daytime versus nighttime, or weekdays versus weekends.

Establishing Criteria for Formulating Your Target Markets

After compiling the market characteristics in the preceding formats, you need to organize your selected market configurations. This is done by taking the various market combinations and selecting one or several target markets to pursue. First, break down your market data into several groups, or target markets, by selecting criteria made up of the market segmentation variables and their corresponding counts. Depending on the product, each profile will contain as many different variables as necessary. For example, if you are marketing toilet paper, your variables will be product usage, demographics/socioeconomics with selected descriptors. On the other hand, if your product is a luxury automobile, you will include lifestyle and psychographic variables. The result is a defined market profile, such as the following example using the CPP/service industry.

Group 1	Counts
Ages: 45–49	2,678
Annual household income: $30,000–39,000	1,709

Prioritization and Selection

Once you complete this process, you will assess each defined market profile's attractiveness. Once again, citing your market segmentation descriptors, you will rank or rate each target market in order of importance. This is accomplished by building criteria and assessing a value to each line item that makes up the criteria. You will go through each market profile and score them to arrive at totals that indicate where the most favorable market can be prioritized and then selected.

Once selected, you then stratify a market or groups of markets into primary, secondary, or tertiary markets. The top markets are primary, the borderline markets are secondary, and the undesirable markets are tertiary. Now that you have completed your target market definition, you need to establish your niche definition—a narrative summary that establishes your mission and direction.

When segmenting a market, you are dividing your area into smaller, more manageable areas. Target marketing is the process of selecting and identifying the market(s) you will view and in which you will ultimately market your products. To understand the differences between a segment and a target market, review Exhibit 1-4.

If you have selected a mass-market definition, the following sections in Unit 1 will not have the same importance as if you had selected a segmented market. Nonetheless, you should follow the steps outlined here to determine your

Exhibit 1-4

Market Focus

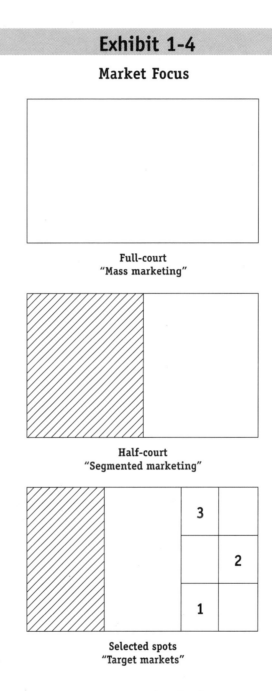

Full-court
"Mass marketing"

Half-court
"Segmented marketing"

Selected spots
"Target markets"

target market management. Formats 8 and 9 display CPP/service examples. IMB industry would use these formats by displaying SIC codes by desired data points (i.e., number of employees, sales volume, etc.).

Market Size Determination

Each identified target market must be defined by its size in a quantified format. The market size is divided into two levels, or variables. The first variable is called

Format 8

Target Market Formulation

		Target Market		
1		**2**		**3**
Descriptors	**Counts**	**Descriptors**	**Counts**	
Males	2,648,594	Males	9,846,575	
Age 20–24	4,446,509	Age 45–49	3,657,300	
White	2,367,444	Hispanic	5,674,974	
Total	345,346		234,562	

Totals represent cross-tabbed totals among descriptors, not total counts of descriptors.

Format 9

Evaluating the Attractiveness of Each Profile Segment

		Target Market		
1		**2**		**3**
Qualify				
Descriptors	**Counts**	**Descriptors**	**Counts**	
Males		Males		
Age 20–24		Age 45–49		
White		Hispanic		
Total	345,346		234,562	
		Target Market		
3(#1)		**2(#2)**		**1(#3)**
Prioritize				
Descriptors	**Counts**	**Descriptors**	**Counts**	
Males		Males		
Age 45–49		Age 45–49		
White		Hispanic		
Total	234,562		147,654	

the *market potential*; its purpose is to establish the maximum dollar or unit amount of a product line available to all firms within a specific defined area and period of time. It is the largest possible description of market size. The second variable is called the *market forecast*; its purpose is to establish the estimated dollar or unit sales of a product or product line for all firms within a certain defined area and period of time. In other words, market potential is units that *could* be sold, and market forecast is units that *should* be sold. (See Format 10.)

One way to find the market forecast is to add up the competition's year-end sales numbers. Remember to include your own sales figures if you are already in the market you are sizing. When figuring your market forecast, ask yourself where you are in relation to that market. If you are considering entering the market, then do not include your sales forecast. If it is a market you are currently in, then do include your sales forecast.

Develop market-size models for the total market area as well as each target market. The full market-size model is completed upon establishing your product's sales potential, sales forecasts, and market share. The model should display data that is linked to your products; this gives the reader a point of reference. For product profitability reasons, you need to know how you might rate against the marketplace.

Format 10

Market Potential and Market Forecast ($ thousands)

Last Three Years	19__ $	19__ Units	19__ $	19__ Units	Rate of Growth (%)	19__ $	19__ Units	Rate of Growth (%)
Market Potential								
Overall	$5,760	2,880	$6,400	3,200	11	$7,040	3,520	11
Product								
Product								
Market Forecast								
Overall	$575	315	$630	350	11	$780	420	20
Product								
Product								

continued

Format 10 (continued)

Market Potential and Market Forecast ($ thousands)

Next Three Years	19___ $	Units	19___ $	Units	Rate of Growth (%)	19___ $	Units	Rate of Growth (%)
Market Potential								
Overall								
Product								
Product								
Market Forecast								
Overall								
Product								
Product								

Market Share and Penetration Measurement

All markets, mass or segmented, have parameters that must be understood in order to enter and/or exist in a market. Direction and size must be quantified to determine where the market is headed in terms of the various shares claimed by current competitors and by the borders of the market itself. If you have already posted year-end sales figures, you can estimate your present and projected market share. Market share should be defined by each target market, by individual products, and by overall product line.

Barriers to Entry

Very few markets exist into which marketers can introduce products quickly and painlessly. Each market has hurdles a business must master to enter and survive. One such hurdle is the market's structure. Its limitations establish what you can and cannot do in that arena. The other is learning how those limitations translate into problems that you will need to resolve.

Every market has limitations. For example, there may be specific time periods in which a product or service is required by the customer. A physical limitation, such as a faulty distribution channel, may also exist. In any case, the marketer needs to identify these limitations and determine their impact in the marketplace. If the limitations can be minimized or eliminated, it may be beneficial to take on the task. This requires careful consideration of both the benefits of opening the marketplace further and the liabilities of going through such a process. In effect, you must ask yourself if the positive results of overcoming barriers outweigh the negative elements that occur while attempting to do so.

Market Share Direction

The next step in defining how you could impact the marketplace is to learn how much room for growth there is in the market. This means that you will address who owns the market and what they represent in terms of market share relative to the competition. The best way to understand how this works is through the example of dividing a pie. How is the pie cut? How many people want a slice? How big is the complete pie? Does each slice of the pie get larger, smaller, fluctuate between the two, or stay the same? The result is determining what you can expect out of the marketplace in terms of what is left.

For example, if you enter into a market and create market share, you will probably take market share either from a current competitor or from the remaining marketplace—more likely the market. When addressing market share, you need to look at it by product, customer type (new, former, and current customers), and geographic area. To analyze anticipated growth, examine growth rates and patterns within the existing market. The objective is to measure fluctuation between the market area that is open for expansion and the collective market shares of your competitors. If the individual or collective market share is declining, the open area in your marketing pie will increase. This means more opportunity for your own growth. If the existing market participants are maintaining or increasing their shares of the pie, your product or service will have less of an opportunity to control a share of the market. Exhibit 1-5 illustrates this concept.

Exhibit 1-5

Market Share Direction

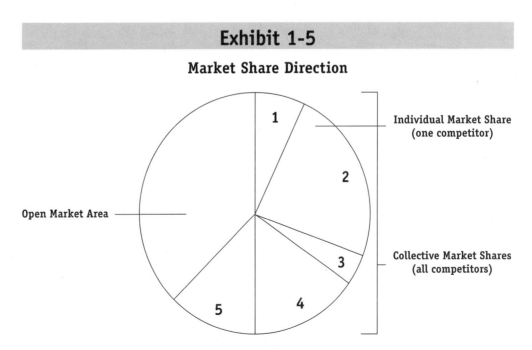

Market Saturation Point

In addition to examining growth rates, you need to determine the *market saturation point*. This point is reached when the combined market shares of all competitors exhaust the market potential. You are not particularly concerned about where a product is in its life cycle at this point—you simply want to know when the availability of the market is likely to end. Format 11 will help you determine market saturation point. It is suggested that you look at five-year time periods for approximately 20 years. In some cases, the lifetime of a market may only be five years total. You can report your data in this model in terms of dollars or market percentage. Be sure to present the rationale upon which you figured your numbers to lend credibility to your estimates.

Format 11						
Market Saturation Point as Indicated by Sales ($)						
	Years					
	5	10	15	20	25	Total
Overall						
Product	$1,000,000	$2,000,000	$1,500,000	$500,000	$1,000	
Product						

Market Penetration Versus Market Share

Normally, when measuring their market share, analysts compare themselves to their competitors (true market share). People like this method because it will produce large percentages even if you are a small player. A more accurate analysis of your market share, however, is to look at a comparison to the entire market. This will give you lower percentages but will be a better indicator of growth potential. Of course, a market audit based on both of these methods is the best choice. When you compare yourself to the entire market, the entire market is called *market penetration*. When someone asks what is your degree of market penetration, you can state that you are a certain percentage of the entire market represented. Format 12 will help you look at market share relative to the entire market and to the competition.

Key Market Factor Assessment

In assessing the entire market structure, it is important to understand its movements and changes. Market factors tell you how the competition is positioned, alert you to risks that the market brings, establish where the market is in its life

Format 12

Market Share

Last Three Years	19___ Units	19___ Units	Rate of Growth (%)	19___ Units	Rate of Growth (%)
Market Share (Relative to Market)					
Overall	5%	1%		6%	3%
Product					
Product					
Market Share (Relative to Competition)					
Overall	43%	6%		47%	7%
Product					
Product					

Next Three Years ($ thousands)	20___ Units	20___ Units	Rate of Growth (%)	20___ Units	Rate of Growth (%)
Market Share (Relative to Market)					
Overall					
Product					
Product					
Market Share (Relative to Competition)					
Overall					
Product					
Product					

$$\text{Market share relative to market} = \frac{\text{Year-End Sales}}{\text{Market Potential}} \qquad \text{Example:} \quad \frac{500}{100,000} = .50\%$$

$$\text{Market share relative to competition} = \frac{\text{Year-End Sales}}{\text{Market Potential}} \qquad \text{Example:} \quad \frac{500}{1,000} = 50\%$$

cycle, and identify sales fluctuations that have occurred because of changes in the marketplace. They address the forces that cause patterns, trends, and flow to materialize from year to year.

Market Positioning

The purpose of *market positioning* is to determine how competitors are placed in the marketplace. Competitors' products are positioned in the marketplace based on their perception of the customer's wants and needs. These wants and needs are translated into market attributes. There are several methods marketers can use to determine what market attributes to look at in analyzing competitors' positioning strategies. Regardless of which one you select, it must match the needs and wants of the customers. Possible strategies include positioning by usage, competition (pricing), alternatives, association, or matching (target market). When collecting your research data regarding customer perceptions of currently available products, be sure to include the influencing factors that will determine that attributes used in the model.

Format 13 is a perceptual map designed to demonstrate positioning of products in your market. In this case, you are concerned with how competitors' products are positioned in the market as judged by factors of customer preference or perceptions. The four sides represent product attributes: expensive/inexpensive, high quality/low quality. The numbers on the vertical and horizontal axes represent customer ranking of product desirability from a low of 1 to a high of 10. The letters A to H represent eight competitors currently in the marketplace. As you analyze these results, it becomes clear that Competitor F is in the best position because its product is relatively inexpensive and high in quality. Both product desirability characteristics are rated well by customers.

The perceptual map method allows you to see how customers' perceive current offerings and highlights areas where your product may fit in the marketing mix. Remember, it is not what you think that counts, it is what the customer perceives that will ensure your spot in the marketplace.

Quality	Price	Competitor
4	3	A
2	1	B
5	6	C
10	4	D
1	10	E
8	7	F
5	3	G
1	4	H

Format 13

Market Positioning

Next Three Years Only

20___

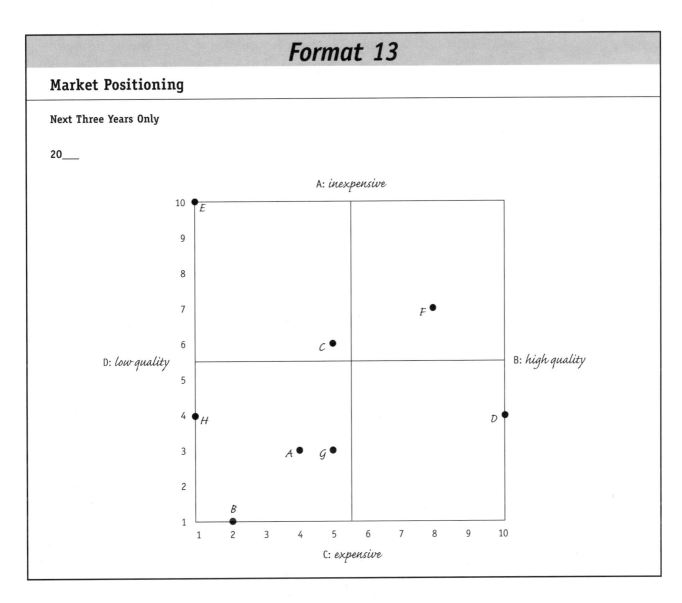

Summary of Key Risks

Each market has an element of risk. Your main objective is to translate a subjective situation into an objective determination of your chances of success or failure. The preferred method is to assess the market's risks by establishing development scenarios that may or may not materialize, based on a set of assumptions that are linked to changing variables or risk factors.

Market Life Cycle

Markets, like products, progress through life cycles. With markets, the stages of the life cycle are the same; it is the factors causing the markets to move through the various stages that differ. These factors are time and customer availability, rather than sales. The other component to be addressed is a market's health, principally in financial terms. If a market is experiencing turmoil, it is less desirable.

There are four life cycle stages for markets:

- introduction (new market/slow growth)

- growth (recognized market/strong growth)

- maturity (utilized market/steady growth)

- decline (low-value market/weak growth)

Depending upon your needs, any one of the market life cycle stages can be attractive to you and beneficial for your particular product.

Use Format 14 to summarize markets from the past three years to the next three years.

Format 14			
Market Life Cycle			
20___			
Product	**Market**	**Life Cycle Stage**	**Health**
Brand X	#1	Growth	Stable
Brand Y	#2	Decline	Unstable

Market Fluctuations

Practically every market has some cycling due to seasonal changes or to economic, cultural, or political events. Your goal is to establish how and to what degree they affect a market's sales performance levels. This will allow you to predict sales peaks and valleys. By charting market fluctuations, you can track changes in the marketplace and in purchasing patterns. Such a chart might look like the one in Format 15. You can also use this format to overlap sales data from your product in order to compare market sales patterns.

Format 15

Sales Cycles: Plot Normal Patterns

20___

Number of Orders/ Sales	Jan.	Feb.	March	April	May	June	July	Aug.	Sept.	Oct.	Nov.	Dec.
10												
9												
8												
7												
6												
5												
4												
3												
2												
1												
0												

Identification of Marketing Industry Standards

Determining the market's marketing standards is a key part of the audit. In doing so, you establish a point of reference as to how things are currently being run. If the standards being used are successful, there is little reason to reinvent the wheel. If the standards are unsuccessful, then perhaps new marketing strategies and tactics could be formed.

These standards are set by companies who compete for business and by regulations and other restrictions. They are the collective standards (shown as averages) of all competitors or those governing bodies. In evaluating the standards or averages, it is important to determine not only what type of activities are being used, but also how effective they are. From these standards you can establish past, present, and future trends by examining the past three years and the next three years. You particularly want to determine market growth rates and why they change.

Marketing Research

The first step in identifying industry standards is to look at trends in the use of marketing research. Your analysis should include marketing research activities (what you are doing now), product research activities (e.g., customer testing), and functional research activities (e.g., media tracking or customer satisfaction studies). Include the following in this section:

- budgets allocated

- research performed

- data collection and processing used

- database usage and management

- results in the marketplace

Product Management and Development

You will also need to determine industry standards and trends in the management of product development. This section should explore strategies used in offering products to the marketplace, including the following elements:

- budgets allocated

- existing product line tactics used

- new product line tactics used

- branding tactics used (if consumer packaged product or service industries)

- packaging used (if consumer packaged product or service industries)

Pricing

Next you will need to determine industry standards and trends in pricing policies. Your inquiry should include acceptable price levels, pricing incentives such as volume discounts and gross margins, reasons for pricing changes, the frequency of such changes, control over costs, and historical pricing patterns. Be sure to include:

- budgets allocated

- price formulas used

- pricing strategies used (i.e., discounting, rebating, etc.)

- price/cost/profit structure

The model in Format 16 allows you to examine industry pricing averages. (Later, in the Competitor Analysis section, you will identify specific price structures.) To use the model, select a series of product types similar to yours that are competing in the market. Call one Product A and another Product B. Then establish the average volume discount programs for each product. For example, is there a 10 percent discount for 1–3 units, a 20 percent discount for 4–10 units, etc.?

Format 16				
Industry Pricing Averages: Profitability and Policy Structure				
	Product: *A*		Product: *B*	
Volume (Units)	1–5	6–10	1–5	6–10
Base price ($)	500	500		
Discount ($)	0	10		
Revenue ($)	500	490		
Costs ($)	200	200		
Gross profit ($)	300	290		
Gross profit margin (%)	60	59		

Based on the volume discount information and the average base price of the product, you can then figure the volume discount average, revenue, and costs of goods sold. The final two lines of the model provide a place for you to determine the average gross profit in dollars and the gross profit margin as a percentage.

Distribution

You will also need to determine industry standards and trends in the use of distribution channels. These include the recognized avenues used in delivering products to the customer or the sales outlet. Items such as transportation and distribution/marketing methods such as sales incentives and dealer financial and support packages need to be established. Be sure to include:

- budgets allocated
- channels used
- delivery systems used

Sales Management

The next step is to investigate industry standards and trends in selling methods and in managing sales. This area of inquiry should focus on the activities employed to generate sales, such as the length of sales cycle, types of sales forces used, sales tools and visual aids used in selling, sales incentives, territory design, and compensation/quota plans. Include the following items in this section:

- budgets allocated

- size of sales force used

- internal sales promotions used

- compensations/quota plans used

- territories configured

Advertising

You will also need to ascertain industry standards and trends in advertising. Included in this area should be media spending (with whom and how much), messages used, media used to communicate the message, reach/frequency/coverage, and principal influences. Be sure to include:

- budgets allocated

- message or themes used

- media used

Format 17 examines the advertising standards by media type.

Format 17			
Advertising Standards: Name and/or Types of Media			
	20___	20___	20___
Direct:			
Mail	60% $130,000*		
Phone			
Cable TV			
Interactive TV			
Video			
Fax			
Computer			

continued

Format 17 (continued)

Advertising Standards: Name and/or Types of Media

	20___	20___	20___
Outdoor			
Billboard			
General signage			
Transit			
Television			
Cable			
Broadcast			
Home shopping	30% $1,000,000		
Infomercials			
Radio			
Spot			
Print			
Newspaper			
Magazine			
Insert (FSI)			
Brochures			
Yellow Pages			
Total	100% $_____	100% $_____	100% $_____

*Enter the percent of total advertising dollars being spent followed by the amount spent for the particular media used.

Promotion Trends

The next step is to determine industry standards and trends regarding promotions. These include activities such as sales promotion spending, sponsorships used, trade shows attended, and event participation. Be sure to include:

- budgets allocated

- message or theme used

- activities and events used

Use Format 18 to collect this information for the last three years and the next three years:

Format 18			
Promotion Standards: Name and/or Types of Media			
	20___	20___	20___
Campaigns			
Sports			
Community projects			
Sponsorship			
Event	10% $1,800,000*		
Place			
Individual			
Merchandising			
Endorsements/licensing			
Catalog			
Sales promotions (for customers)			
Floor displays			
POP			
Rebates/coupons			
Special			
Tradeshows			
Total	100% $_____	100% $_____	100% $_____

*Enter the percent of total advertising dollars being spent followed by the amount spent for each type of activity.

Public Relations

You will also need to establish industry standards and trends for public relations. Included in this area should be activities such as techniques used for promoting positive images, as well as publicity and media relations policies. Be sure to include:

- budgets allocated

- message or theme used

- media strategies used

- activities or events used

Legal Issues

You will need to assess the industry standards and trends for legal activities such as proper positioning on legislative issues, relations with government agencies, and monitoring and influencing legislation. Be sure to include:

- budgets allocated

- laws or regulations monitored

Customer Service

The final step in this section is to determine the industry standards and trends as they relate to customer service and support. With customer management being paramount in any marketing plan today, how customers are treated and how they impact a company's marketing efforts are key. The industry should address the following items:

- customer satisfaction surveys

- customer partnering

- customer help lines

Indentifying Secondary Target Markets

Earlier, we discussed how markets are prioritized and selected. The question is, what do you do with the other markets, especially the secondary markets? Secondary markets develop because of primary market resource limitations, new market growth, and organizational challenges. They present a business opportunity. As a result, after you select your primary market, you should identify secondary or alternative markets. Segment numbers in Formats 19–21 represent market profiles selected in Formats 9 and 10.

Defining Secondary Target Markets by Product

To define a secondary market for future consideration by product, select a desired profile segment by defined trade areas, using the product as a method for additional market penetration. Record your data in Format 19.

Defining Secondary Target Markets by Geography

To define a secondary market for future consideration by geographic area, select a desired profile segment by defined trade areas, using geography as a method for additional market penetration. Record your data in Format 20.

Defining Secondary Target Markets by Customer

To define a secondary market for future consideration by customer type, select a desired profile segment by defined trade areas, using customer type as a method for additional market penetration. Record your data in Format 21.

Formats 19, 20, and 21			
Defining Secondary Target Markets			
	Segment (Market Profile)		
	1	2	3	4
Secondary			
Tertiary			

Customer Profiling

The centerpiece of the market audit, and therefore the marketplace, is the customer. In the consumer packaged product and service industries, the customer is the end user of the product. Yes, you could say that a drugstore or supermarket is the customer, but it is really your partner; the customer is the end consumer of that product. In the industrial manufacturing/business-to-business industry, the customer will be a producer or supplier of a product for the end user.

The customer has always been a key element in building one's marketing processes, but today's customer is the driver for product and marketing management. In fact, customer management has become as important as these two traditional marketing functions. Today, the focus is on customer relationship marketing, emphasizing where a customer is at in the life cycle. This approach presents marketing opportunities and problems. Customer management concentrates on share of the customer, not share of the market. It looks at taking products to the customer, not customers to the product. Up to this point, the customer has been viewed as a number value or a group. Now you are going to put a face on that statistical effort to establish who your customers are.

Identifying Your Customers

Understanding who your customers are, why they buy, where they buy, and how often they buy may be the most important marketing knowledge you ever possess. Marketing is far more exact than people realize, but it will never be completely exact because of the element of human behavior (buyer behavior). This is the most difficult variable to judge and predict. You must identify specifically who your customers will be and then define their needs and wants. Once this is done, you can better determine how to reach them and acquire them as your customers. Once again, you may want to identify these customers by your product or product line to give you a reference point.

In the market segmentation section, segment profiles are established by using various attributes and variables. In the consumer package product industry, you use many of those same components to establish who these customers are, except now you are identifying an actual person, place, or thing, not a profile or cluster. As a result, the customer ID in the market audit means defining the individual types of customers, as either one type or a range of types.

Exhibits 1-6 and 1-7 illustrate how the customer profiling process links with the entire market definition process.

The various industries will call upon you to build your customer profiles by looking at different market dynamics and market data resources. If you are in the consumer package product or service industries, you need to focus on market segmentation and target marketing, customer life cycle, and internal specific database attributes. If you are in the industrial manufacturing/business-to-business industry, your focus should include, market segmentation and target marketing, and customer/channel life cycle.

Format 22 provides you with the framework from which to prioritize the most attractive customers by the profile you have built.

Exhibit 1-6

Market Identification and the Customer Profiling Process

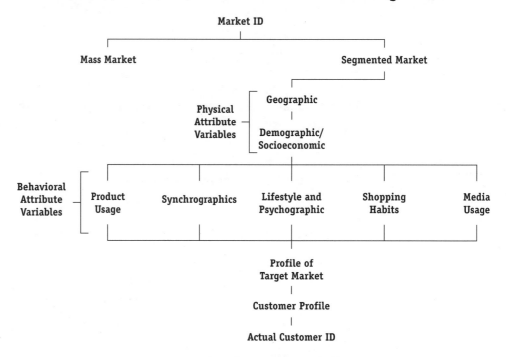

Market ID

Mass Market   Segmented Market

Physical Attribute Variables — Geographic

Demographic/ Socioeconomic

Behavioral Attribute Variables — Product Usage | Synchrographics | Lifestyle and Psychographic | Shopping Habits | Media Usage

Profile of Target Market

Customer Profile

Actual Customer ID

Exhibit 1-7

Market Identification and the Customer Identification Process

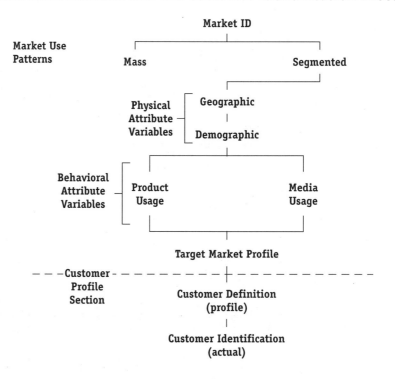

Market ID

Market Use Patterns

Mass   Segmented

Physical Attribute Variables — Geographic

Demographic

Behavioral Attribute Variables — Product Usage | Media Usage

Target Market Profile

— — Customer Profile Section — — — — — — — — — — — —

Customer Definition (profile)

Customer Identification (actual)

Format 22				
Customer Definition				
Product				
Target Market	#1		#2	
Customer	Primary	Secondary	Primary	Secondary
Description				
	Hispanic, males, 35–50 yrs. old	Hispanic, males' wives, 35–50 yrs. old	White, males, 35–50 yrs. old	White, males' wives, 35–50 yrs. old

Reasons for Purchase

Once you identify the customers, you have to establish how they make the decision to purchase a product like yours, where and when they are most likely to buy it, how often they buy this product, and how much of it they will buy. Assessing customers' value for a particular product is difficult; the trick is identifying how the product satisfies a need or solves a problem. Once you determine that, you can evaluate the customers' purchasing power by measuring how often they make purchases; this information can help you predict sales fluctuations. You should also analyze customers' purchase decision process and what influences their purchases. (See Exhibits 1-8 and 1-9.)

If you are in the consumer package product or service industries, the ultimate goal is to measure customers' shopping patterns by where they shop and link this information with what they buy and why. It is important to identify where shopping activities occur, whether near customers' workplaces or residential neighborhoods. If you are in the industrial manufacturing/business-to-business industry, the ultimate goal is to measure customers' buying habits and link this information with what they buy and why.

Identifying Needs and Wants

There are many important elements to consider in defining the marketplace, but the bottom line is customer needs. Whether or not customers' needs are currently being satisfied, or if they are ready to have a need created for them, remember that customer needs are your number-one priority. The key elements in measuring need are customers' level of satisfaction and what motivates them to make purchases (quality, price, etc.).

A *need* is usually a requirement for living (e.g., food and shelter) A *want* is more often a desire to possess something that is not required for daily living or is a deluxe version of a minimum standard. It is important to understand the category your product falls under. This will help to shape your product features and benefits and your marketing activities in reaching the customer.

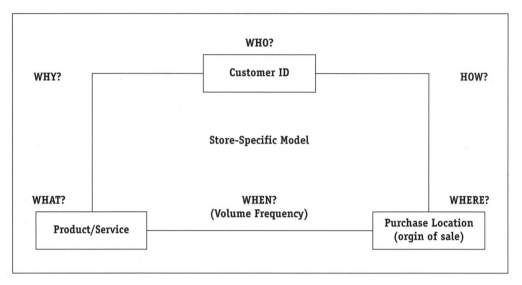

Exhibit 1-8

Identifying Product Purchased and Product Location

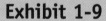

Exhibit 1-9

Customer Model

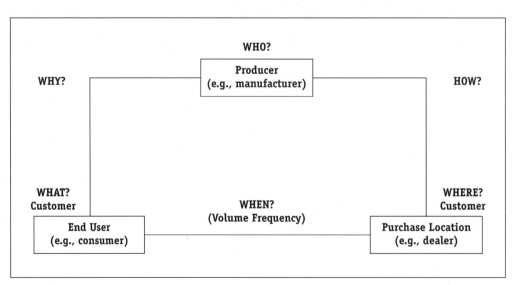

Problem Identification

Once you understand the customers' needs, you need to define why a need exists and how long it will last. The main point to understand, once again, is why a customer does or does not buy. In addition, what are the alternatives a customer could exercise in deciding whether or not to purchase? What are actual or potential solutions to problems?

Buying Behavior

The next step in defining customer factors is to understand and perhaps predict the element of buyer behavior. It is this element that causes marketing to be an inexact science; no matter how strong your marketing efforts are, the customer still has the ultimate power in deciding to buy. A key measurement of behavior is how much of a product a customer uses. The heavier the use level, the easier it is to understand customers' buying habits. The buying behavior to be charted includes:

- frequency of purchase (consumption patterns)

- volume of purchase

- circumstances of purchase (e.g., reorders)

- overall purchasing power (e.g., available resources)

- purchases made during a selected time period

Customer purchasing power measures the ability of an individual or group to generate sales. The model in Format 23 will allow you to track customer purchasing performance for the last three and the next three years. For both primary and secondary markets, rate purchasing performance by frequency (how often a purchase is made) and by volume (how many units are purchased). You can then rate customer performance by either criterion or both.

Format 23

Frequency and Volume of Purchases by Priority Customers

20___

Product

Customer ID	Frequency		Volume	
	Low	High	Low	High
1. *Primary*		X—————————	————————— X	
2. *Secondary*		X————— X		

Understanding the Purchase Decision Process

Now you are ready to isolate the actual act of purchasing. Although it is impossible to truly understand the final moments before a customer decides to purchase products, the process can be tracked and projected to some extent. The process a customer goes through when selecting a product is especially important in the consumer package product industry, where branding comes into play. Branding gives products an identity and gives the customer more options and issues to consider. Once you determine why they buy and when they buy, your understanding of how customers think about the product can be manipulated to impact favorably on a product purchase.

Elements in understanding the purchase decision process include:

- length of sales cycle (how long does it take customers to buy?)

- impulse, planned, loyal, and complex purchase decisions (as shown in Format 24-1)

- timing (e.g., seasonal)

Format 24-1

Purchasing Decision Variables

Brand Product

	Impulse (%)	Planned (%)	Loyal (%)	Complex (%)	Total (%)
1. Primary	25%	25%	25%	25%	100%
2. Primary	30	40	20	10	100
3. Secondary	40	10	40	10	100
4. Secondary	35	15	40	10	100

Although Format 24-2 should be used for industrial manufacturing/business-to-business industry, many of the items contained in this format can be applied in the consumer package product or service industries. This format was designed for customers who are producers or suppliers of products. The following definitions will aid you in building the purchase decision process.

- Length of sales cycle: How long does it take the customer to buy?

- Timing: Does the time of the year impact the customer's purchase?

- Approach: Is it planned or response driven?

- Stability: Can you depend on them?

- Knowledge: Do they require information, directions, and assistance?

- Payment system: What is the method of payment (cash, credit, terms, etc.)?

- Attitude: Are they conservative, moderate or liberal in the amount of the purchase?

- Structure: Are purchase decisions made by a department, a person, or on-line means?

Format 24-2

Purchasing Decision Variables

Product: ABC Product

Variable	Response
Length of sales cycle	*6 months*
Timing	*June only*
Approach	*Planned*
Stability	*Unorganized*
Knowledge	*Learning*
Payment System	*Credit*
Attitude	*Traditional*
Structure	*Privately held*

Purchasing Influences

With each purchase, something or someone influences a customer's decision to obtain or not to obtain a product. The trick is to identify the forces that govern the decision-making process. Once you do that, you can assess how complex the market is. The more elements that impact a decision to purchase, the more difficult it will be to effectively control that market in terms of time, effort, and money. Types of purchasing influences to consider include:

- individual/group/parent/peer opinions

- price sensitivity

- personal preferences

- source of product information (e.g., media, friends, etc.)

In addition, you need to define how customers buy, consume, and rebuy products. A customer can be an initiator, influencer, decider, purchaser, or user. A customer can be one or all of those things, or others can be part of the customer's buying process. The key is to isolate who is making the decision to buy and what roles other actions play in the buying process. The result will ultimately be a marketing plan that is aware of all elements of the buying process so as to influence those actions to secure the sale.

Origin of Sale (Consumer Package Product and Service Industries Only)

Origin of sale is a key element in purchase motivation because at that point an individual makes the final decision to buy, seeks out the product, and makes the transaction. Analyzing the origin of sale tells you why, where, and when customers are purchasing your products and what the most effective placement would be. Be sure to consider the following in your audit:

- point of purchase origin (type of store, outlet, Internet access, etc.)

- point of delivery (if separate)

- point of product sale (motivation)

The origin of sale model in Format 25 can be completed with research or scanner data that you have already obtained. Your objective here is to establish why customers buy and then match that data to your consumer types. For example, if you are relying on primary market research in the form of a survey, you could ask consumers to rank motivating factors on a scale from 1 to 5. If price was not a strong incentive to buy, the consumer would rank that factor as 1.

To indicate customer purchase motivation patterns, select the element that most likely motivates a customer by placing a number between 1 and 10 (10 being the strongest) to determine importance. Once you determine why a customer makes the decision to buy, you can identify where he or she completes the purchase. Format 26 displays where customers shop according to type of store.

Format 25

Customer Purchase Motivation

Product	Motivation to Buy				
	Price	Selection	Service	Quality/Appearance	Location
1. Primary	1	4	2	3	5
2. Primary	5	3	2	1	4
3. Secondary	3	2	1	5	4

Format 26

Customer Sales*

Last Three Years/Next Three Years

20___

| Product: _____ | Customer Type | | | | | |
| | Primary | | | Secondary | | |
	dollars	units	%	dollars	units	%
Retail						
Discount store	$3,000	1,000	10	$2,000	667	12
Department store	8,000	2,667	30	5,000	1,667	40
Specialty store	4,000	1,333	40	1,000	333	8
Variety store						
Supermarket						
Catalog showroom						
Convenience store						
Wholesale						
Warehouse showroom						
Industrial distributors						
Special						
Mail order						
Brokers						
Automatic/vending						
Door-to-door						
TV shopping						

*Dollars shown in millions

After you establish why and where a customer tends to buy, you can pinpoint where the purchasing behavior occurs. A method called *store-specific analysis* uses new technology to help you track products based on the specific locations at which they were purchased. This information is generally obtained through scanner data vendors and can be recorded as shown in Format 27.

Format 27

Store-Specific Performance (Origin/Point of Sale)

Product/Brand	Customer Type/Composite	Store Location
Toothpaste/Crest	Primary	XYZ Market/10th & Main
Butter/Store's	Primary	XYZ Market/10th & Main
Soda/Canada Dry	Secondary	Fred's Market/32 E. Doe St.

You can now take the store you have identified and determine its trade/service area. Your first objective is to break down the area by priority markets and then match the address of the customer with the store location. This should help you determine if the connection between customer and location is based on the neighborhood or on the attraction to a specific store. (See Format 28.) Remember, the more specific you can be about geographic levels, the more accurate your analysis becomes.

The bottom line is to focus on the decision makers—the customers who will buy the product or service you are marketing. They will represent a profile (driven from the market segmentation/target market or company database) that will reveal their buying habits. These customers will fall into one of the following categories:

- household-based

- individual-based

- business-based (place of work)

Format 28

Store-Specific Location (Market/Trade Area)

Store/Location	Defined Areas		
	Primary Block Level	Secondary Block Level	Tertiary Block Level
XYZ Market, 106 Main	38 blocks, 183 primary customers		
XY2 Market, 104 Main			
Fred's Market, 32 E. Doe St.			

Origin of Sale (Industrial Manufacturing/ Business-to-Business Only)

Origin of sale is a key element in purchase motivation because at this point an individual makes the final decision to buy, seeks out the product, and makes the actual transaction. Analyzing the origin of sale tells you the reasoning behind the purchase of a product.

In this industry, the decision maker is defined not by household, residence, or place of work, but by the position and level of authority within a company. The following structure displays where decision makers can exist. This allows you to isolate and identify your most likely customers.

Decision Makers—By Department Type

1. Engineering

    - manufacturing engineers

    - design engineers

    - plant engineers and management

    - research and development personnel

    - chemists

2. Production and manufacturing

    - maintenance

    - production

    - safety

    - warehousing and transportation

3. Operations

    - corporate/business unit management

    - administration

    - marketing and sales

    - finance and accounting

    - customer service and support

    - technology/data/MIS management

4. Purchasing

    - agents

    - buyers

Decision Makers—By Operational Control

1. Corporate/business unit level

   - president/owner

   - vice president

2. Operational level

   - director

   - senior manager

3. Department/functional level

   - department manager/head

   - project coordinator

4. Employee/staff level

   - area supervisor

   - line/field staffer

   - analyst

Customer Identification

At this point, total customer identification is possible by matching the customer identification and reasons for purchase (customer profile) with a customer database (current and potential) to create a customer list for marketing purposes. To perform this match, compare your desired customer (as listed on Format 22, Customer Definition) with a list of actual customers from your database. Format 29 can be used for this comparison and should serve as a basis for your data file.

The example in Format 29 reflects the consumer package product or service industry customer profile. For the industrial manufacturing/business-to-business industry, the customer profile would reflect the SIC code (or equivalent classification), as well as the name (department and control), company name, and address (including phone, fax, and Internet address).

When you are through building the composite sketch of your most likely customers, you need to be able to answer the following questions:

- Who are they?

- What do they do with it?

- Where do they buy it?

- When do they buy it?

Format 29	

Customer ID Data File

Customer Profile Type	Actual Customer
1. Customer variables	1. Customer
a. Hispanic	a. Address: *163 Hillside Dr., Chicago, IL 60621*
b. Males	b. Customer name: *Pedro Valdez*
c. 35–50 years old	c. Telephone number: *312-555-0000*
2. Customer variables	1. Customer
a. White	a. Address:
b. Males	b. Customer name:
c. 35–50 years old	c. Telephone number:

- Why do they buy it?
- How do they buy it?

Customer Marketability

One of the key issues to address is the cost to reach, capture, and maintain a customer, and the price he or she is willing to pay for your product or service. The customer costing aspect is important because it establishes a customer's real level of attractiveness. For example, a customer may be perfectly suited for your product or service, but the efforts or resources needed to obtain and keep that customer are so great that he or she is not worth pursuing. Costs can include advertising, direct marketing (cost per lead), and sales and promotion, to name a few. The pricing aspect (already discussed) is also part of this equation. You need to determine, along with cost and sales volume/frequency, the price level you can charge a customer. Once you estimate the level of customer profitability, you can assess how marketable a customer is and calculate the risk and return a customer may generate.

Essentially you are summing up the findings in your audit to this point and determining what it will take to market to a given customer type. This will include the remaining portion of the Unit 1 exercises as well.

Competitor Analysis

Understanding your competitors' capabilities, resources, and strategies can help you pinpoint their vulnerabilities. Competition can manifest itself in many ways, such as a high-tech company that invents a new product for a new need. Although the need is new or there may be no other competitors in the marketplace, chances are that a customer is filling the need in some other way. You should also remember to identify competitors at different levels. For example, if you are an airline carrier, your competition is not only other airline carriers, but also all other forms of transportation.

Identifying Your Competition

It is important to discover as much information as possible about your competition, but that may prove difficult because competitors do not freely share meaningful information. Complete the following formats to the best of your ability with the information at hand.

The model in Format 30 provides a method for identifying your competitors by product line and target market. Be sure to identify products at the various points of their life cycle. If they are in decline, they should be listed in the "Past" column. Active products go in the "Present" column. Products that are under development or have not yet reached market are classified as "Future."

Format 30

Competitor Identification

Competitor	Past	Present	Future	Target Market/Customers
ABC Company		Brand X		20–35-year-old white females
XYZ, Inc.			Brand Y	35–50-year-old white females

(Product Line spans Past, Present, Future)

Format 31 identifies competitors by performance power in the marketplace. Identify each competitor by area of distribution (local, national, regional) and market share (in percent). Then rank them in order of importance to the market.

A third way to identify competitors is by sales and market share performance. You must first establish sales levels by looking at two variables: sales potential and sales forecast. *Sales potential* is based on the resources of a competitor and its ability to use those resources to meet the needs of its service area. *Sales forecast* is a measure of their current sales projections for coming years. When using either variable, examine current and past projections to gauge how well a competitor met its expectations. Use Formats 32 and 33 for this analysis.

Format 31

Competition by Target Market

Competitor	Ranking	Market Share	Distribution
Brand X	1st	50%	National
Brand Y	2nd	20	National

Format 32

Competitor Sales Performance ($ thousands)

Last Three Years	19__ $	19__ Units	19__ $	19__ Units	Rate of Growth (%)	19__ $	19__ Units	Rate of Growth (%)
Sales Potential								
Overall	$100	1,000	$150	1050	5%	$200	1200	14%
Product								
Product								
Sales Forecast								
Overall	60	600	85	850	42	120	999	18
Product								
Product								

continued

Measuring the Competition's Strengths and Weaknesses

Once you establish who the players are in the marketplace and what impact they have on that marketplace, you need to assess each one's strengths and weaknesses. In measuring strengths, you will need to determine five basic elements that can give you a profile of what competitors are doing well now and what they can do to better themselves in the future:

Format 32 (continued)

Competitor Sales Performance ($ thousands)

Next Three Years	19___ $	Units	19___ $	Units	Rate of Growth (%)	19___ $	Units	Rate of Growth (%)
Sales Potential								
Overall								
Product								
Product								
Sales Forecast								
Overall								
Product								
Product								

Format 33

Competitor Market Share ($ thousands)

Last Three Years	19___ Units	19___ Units	Rate of Growth (%)	19___ Units	Rate of Growth (%)
Market Share (Relative to Market)					
Overall	8%	8%		9%	
Product	4%	5%		6%	
Product	4%	3%		3%	
Market Share (Relative to Competition)					
Overall	50%	50%		55%	
Product	29%	30%		33%	
Product	25%	20%		22%	

continued

Format 33 _(continued)_					
Competitor Market Share ($ thousands)					
Next Three Years	**20__** Units	**20__** Units	**Rate of Growth (%)**	**20__** Units	**Rate of Growth (%)**
Market Share (Relative to Market)					
Overall					
Product					
Product					
Market Share (Relative to Competition):					
Overall					
Product					
Product					

- ability to satisfy customers' needs and desires
- track record and reputation
- staying power (financial resources)
- key personnel
- product and target market approach

To this point, the information you have used to identify the competition has been quantitative. Format 34 allows you to write qualitative, narrative information about each competitor's abilities.

In measuring weaknesses, you will try to identify what the competition cannot do well, or at least areas that may be open to problems. Use the same five elements that you used to assess their strengths to achieve a balanced viewpoint.

Use Format 35 to write qualitative narrative descriptions of each competitor's disadvantages.

Evaluating Competitors' Marketing Strategies and Tactics

Another area of focus is competitors' marketing actions. Unlike the marketing mix industry standards section, which collectively measures all competitors, regulators, and customers by establishing industry norms, averages, and ranges, this

Format 34

Competitive Advantages of Competitors

| Competitor | Strengths | | | |
	A	B	C	D
Brand X	Seems to satisfy customer needs moderately. Strength comes as a result of ease of usage, low price, and advertising.	Has a long and strong history of quality. Customers treat it as a reliable old stand-by.	Parent company just went public, giving them a lot of new cash flow.	Product manager has been at her job for 20 years and knows the business.
Brand Y	Satisfies customer needs better than Brand X by being better and faster.	Replacing a product that was very successful. Is new and has a limited track record.	Owned by XYZ, Inc., which is a secure, expanding, family-owned business.	R&D staff is excellent and is always looking to improve products.

Format 35

Competitive Disadvantages of Competitors

| Competitor | Weaknesses | | | |
	A	B	C	D

section deals with each competitor individually and pinpoints each one's approach to marketing.

The first element of measurement is a competitor's level of profitability. Items such as gross profit margins, gross profit/income levels, return on investment, and cost of marketing have to be determined. Your biggest hurdle will be in obtaining this sensitive information, but if you can do so, it will be extremely valuable.

Format 36 can be used to illustrate elements of a competitor's profitability level. Again, you will only be able to use as much of this form as you have information for.

Format 36
Profitability and Financial Structure
20___
Competitor: *Brand X*
Overall Product Line (Year Ending/Past)
Sales ($)   *$200,000*
Sales (units)   *$1,200*
Rate of growth (%)   *14%*
Cost of goods sold   *$100,000*
Gross profit   *$100,000*
Gross margin   *50%*
Product (Year Ending/Future)
Sales ($)
Sales (units)
Rate of growth (%)
Cost of goods sold
Gross profit
Gross margin

It sounds overly simplified, but if a product can't be produced and sold at a price that covers cost of production, generates profit, and is attractive to customers, it is unmarketable. In analyzing your competition's ability to sell a marketable product, you need to know their cost and price structuring. Format 37 is the same as the one you used in the Industry Standards section. Complete it as before, but use information on the competitor's pricing structure.

In analyzing profitability, it is also important to examine marketing expenses. This key component, commonly called *cost of marketing*, or *cost of sales*, is an additional method of viewing a competitor's ability to produce marketable products. Format 38 asks you to identify how much a competitor is spending and how that amount relates to the percent of products sold.

Format 37

Pricing/Cost Structure

20___

Competitor: *Brand X*

	Product			Product	
Volume (Units)	1–5	6–10	11–15	1–5	5+
Price ($)	$167	$167			
Discount ($)	0	20			
Revenue ($)	167	147			
Costs ($)	84	64			
Gross profit ($)	83	63			

Format 38

Marketing Expenses by Competitor

Marketing Function	20___ ($)	Percentage of Total Sales	20___ ($)	Percentage of Total Sales	Percentage Change of Allocated Dollars
Marketing research	5,000	2.5	4,000	2.0	<20.0>
Product/new product development	3,000	1.5	2,000	1.0	<33.3>
Pricing	0	0	0	0	0
Distribution	5,000	2.5	6,000	3.0	20.0
Sales	10,000	5.0	11,000	5.5	10.0
Advertising	8,500	4.3	10,000	5.0	17.7
Promotions	6,000	3.0	8,000	4.0	33.3
Public relations	500	0.3	0	0	<100.0>
Legal	2,000	1.0	1,000	0	<50.0>
Total	40,000	—	42,000	—	5.0
Percentage of sales	20%	20.1%	21%	21.0%	—

Format 39

Media Usage Expenses by Competitor

	20___ ($)	Percent of Total Media Budget	20___ ($)	Percent of Total Media Budget	20___ ($)	Total
Direct response						
Mail	—	—	2,000	20		2,000
Phone	—	—	1,000	10		1,000
Cable TV	—	—	—	—		—
Interactive TV	—	—	—	—		—
Video	—	—	—	—		—
Fax	—	—	—	—		—
Computer	—	—	—	—		—
Outdoor response						
Billboard	—	—	—	—		—
General signage	—	—	—	—		—
Transit	—	—	—	—		—
Television viewership						
Cable	1,500	17.0	1,500	15.0		3,000
Broadcast	—	—	—	—		—
Home shopping	—	—	—	—		—
Infomercials	—	—	—	—		—
Radio listenership						
Spot	4,000	47.0	1,000	10.0		5,000
Print readership						
Newspaper	2,000	24.0	1,000	10.0		3,000
Magazine	—	—	2,000	20.0		2,000
Insert (FSI)	—	—	—	—		—
Yellow Pages	1,000	12.0	1,000	10.0		2,000

continued

Format 39 (continued)

Media Usage Expenses by Competitor

	20___ ($)	Percent of Total Media Budget	20___ ($)	Percent of Total Media Budget	20___ ($)	Total
Special viewership						
Sports	—	—	—	—		0
POP	—	—	500	5.0		500
Floor displays	—	—	—	—		—
Coupons	—	—	—	—		—
Sales premiums	—	—	—	—		—
Total	$8,500	100	$10,000	100.0		$18,500

A media usage expense analysis, shown in Format 39, is a tool to extract the advertising expenses from an overall budget. Advertising costs tabulated on this format should include such things as production and media placement. The data are displayed as a dollar amount and as a percentage of the total advertising budget.

The next step is to find out what new products competitors have in the pipeline research and development and whether there are companies that could become new competitors as a result of new product introductions. (See Format 40.) Once again, obtaining this information is difficult because competitors are even more secretive about these activities than about their profits. However, competitors can usually keep quiet about their products only in the initial stages; once they begin testing their secrets, they become harder to protect.

Format 40

Research and Development Activities

20___

Competitor	Stage	Release Date	Impact
XK-1000	Prototype	June '00	Replacement of product
20001-A	Test market	April '00	All new product

As an extension of the research and development activities section, it is vital to understand how new developments will translate into market opportunities for you. How long will your window of opportunity be open before your initial success breeds new competition? How would competitors' products compare with yours? These are just a few of the issues you need to resolve. Format 41 will help you complete this analysis.

Format 41

Opportunity Projects

20___

New Competitors	Products	Estimated Base Price	Features/Benefits
Top Gun, Inc.	XK-1000	$170	Time-saving
AAAA Corp.	20001-A	200	Multipurpose

As you evaluate the marketplace to determine whether you want to enter it, you also need to assess competitors' ability to enter and survive. Barriers to entering a market are generally linked to cost, especially in terms of investment cost. The goal is to see if competitors are experiencing the barriers you've witnessed and to what degree they are dealing with them. Use Format 42 as a model.

You also need to address your competitors' ability to change. What resources do they possess or could they get access to quickly? Who might be a likely partner? Is funding an issue? When assessing competitors, you need to look at them today and tomorrow in terms of their ability to respond to market changes and other competitors.

Regulatory and Cultural Concerns

Almost every market is regulated in some way. Not understanding the rules of the game and not working within those rules can destroy your marketing efforts. What if you launched a consumer product and discovered after several weeks that a new law was passed or a new technology was licensed that either forced you to retool the product or eliminated it altogether? Such a mistake would prove to be very costly. Knowing what to expect can help you determine the market's future.

Format 42

Competitors' Barriers to Entry

Competitor	A. Time	B. Technology	C. Key Personnel	D. Customer Limitations	E. Existing Patents and Trademarks
Brand X	Their window of opportunity is estimated to be 6 months, beginning 2 months from now. However, they may not be in their new factory in time to produce and bring the product to market.	The technology they are using is outdated and although it works, it will never let Brand X perform at the level it should.	They have very loyal workers who are flexible. The result is that they can be counted on to adjust to market demands in terms of production scheduling.	Customers feel very good about the product and are willing to accept change.	No violation of patents.
Brand Y	Because their product is new, their timing is perfect. They are positioned to hit the ground running.	Brand Y is built on a whole new platform; as a result it is not only able to meet current market needs but can be expanded.	Key people are missing in the service/support area. Without these people, pushing a new product onto the market may create a major problem.	Previous customers of Brand Y were not very loyal. As a result, there is some question if customers will risk trying and using this product on a regular basis.	No violations of patents.

Government Regulations

Most restrictions come from government regulations. A government agency that administers laws, rules, and regulations is set up to control a market and keep it safe and fair for all. Such agencies can have federal, state, or local authority. Your goals are to be aware of all government requirements, to identify the various government agencies that oversee market actions, and to determine your costs of complying. Consider the following elements:

- business licensing

- product approval (e.g., FDA, EPA, etc.)

- tax implications (e.g., IRS, etc.)

- consumer labeling/packaging awareness (e.g., FTC)

- purchase limitations

Laws That Affect the Product's Existence

It is not enough to understand and comply with the present legal situation. You also need to be aware of impending changes to existing laws, rules, and regulations as well as new laws, rules, and regulations that are being considered. Pending legislation can affect a market negatively or positively. Use Format 43 to track these concerns.

Format 43

Laws/Rules/Regulations

Product	Past	Current	Future	Agency/Legislative Control
Your Product 1		x		FTC
Your Product 2		x	x	FDA/FTC

Other Market Limitations

Other limitations stem from factors inherent to the market environment's structure. As shown in Format 44, you will need to identify the various factors that impact the market, analyze their influence, and determine how they can be changed. Be sure to consider:

- economic factors

- cultural factors

- technological factors

- political factors (e.g., associations, unions, quasi-governmental agencies, watchdog groups)

- time factors

- suppliers

- environmental issues

Format 44

Anticipated Market Changes

Product	Factor Type	Effect on Market
Your Product 1	Cultural	Hispanic community acceptance
Your Product 2	Economic	Customers are unemployed/low income

Meeting the Requirements and Making Changes

Once you establish what it will take to conform to the market's requirements, you must then assess what it will cost and whether it is worth the effort and investment to make the necessary adjustments. You will also need to define the options that are open.

Timing Involved in Meeting the Requirements

The time it will take to meet market requirements is very important for projecting costs and resource allocations. How long it takes you to comply with these changes will once again tell you the amount of effort it will take to exist in the marketplace.

Cost of Meeting the Requirements

The cost of meeting market requirements is the bottom-line issue. You should go into great detail to determine how much it will cost in real dollars to comply with requirements before entering the market. Use the model in Format 45.

Format 45			
Cost of Meeting Market Requirements			
Product	**Restriction**	**Timing**	**Cost to Comply**
Your Product 1	Federal law	6 months	$15,000 (filing and legal fees)
Your Product 2	Economic	No limit	Does not apply

Additional Market Audit Applications

The market audit in this situation, is being used to look at one's physical market area to determine how to target customers, produce products, and create marketing actions (a plan). However, you can use the elements offered in the first unit of this book in related applications such as:

- feasibility studies
- cost-benefit analyses
- site analyses
- due diligence for mergers and acquisitions
- business appraisals

Comparing Your Market Audit Findings with Other Published Data

Evaluating Existing Marketing Studies

Many relevant marketing studies have probably been performed for your target markets by competitors, investment bankers, private research firms, and others. If possible, use those research sources to check your findings and to further define the market. Consider these questions in evaluating existing marketing research data:

- Who compiled and published the report?

- When was the study performed?

- How many sources were used?

- Where was the study performed?

- Why was the study conducted, and who paid for it?

- What were the results and who benefited from those results?

- How do the findings compare with your findings?

- Are adjustments needed or should more marketing research be performed?

Adjusting Your Market Audit Findings

After you complete your market audit and compare your findings with other findings, you may need to do more research or go back through your audit and verify your data. It is always best to review other approaches and results to get an objective viewpoint in this very subjective science. (See Format 46.)

Format 46

Additional/Supportive Insight

Product	Previous Marketing Studies	Date	Findings	Adjustments (if any)
Your Product 1	Hopkins research marketing study	2000	Strong value placed on educating consumer	Review legal concerns
Your Product 2	No studies	—	—	—

Measuring Demand

At the end of the market audit, it is important to assess the degree of demand in the marketplace. It is difficult to place a value in a quantitative or qualitative formula. There is almost always a need for a product in every market; the key is recognizing the difference between need and demand. You make money with demand, not need.

Market demand is best defined by combining the following items in a set formula:

- volume and frequency

- length and complexity of sales cycle

- market potential

- competition and alternatives

- general customer presence (recognition of the value of product, willingness to seek out the product, and pay the average price sold for that given product)

The key items are how often, how many, and at what price in a given time frame. Answers to these questions will give you a good gauge of the demand for your products and what it is worth to you as a business.

Unit 2

Defining the Product Line Value

Product and Income Source Profiling

In Unit 1 you defined the market and determined how you wish to attack and manage it. Now you need to define the products and non-product income sources you will offer to that market. It is important to distinguish between these two sources of business or profit centers.

Product Sources

Today, products are still the primary source of business generation. A product is defined as a tangible object or intangible service that can be sold to a customer to be used or consumed and that satisfies one or a series of needs. Products are packaged and sold by offering specific features and benefits. Products can be marketed as a single item or as part of an overall product line. Products are often marketed under a brand name to give them an identity. In fact, many products are marketed with such a huge identity that the company that produces them becomes the products being marketed.

Non-Product Income Sources

Although product-based income still produces the major part of a business's income, in more and more situations, alternative income sources are augmenting a business's ability to meet annual profit goals. These income sources can be service fees, commissions paid, or licensing royalties.

The key point is that income can come from traditional products and non-traditional non-products. As you work through the exercises in this unit, think of how these formats apply not only to traditionally defined products, but to non-products as well.

Product and Customer Management Review

Now that you know you must treat all income sources as products, you must assess the value of those income sources and add the element of the customer to your value assessment. You need to continually reference the customer as you establish the strengths and weaknesses of your current products and possible replacements or additions.

The Customer Element

For the past 100 years, companies have standardized their products and services to take advantage of economies of scale. They have also standardized their marketing actions, and in the process, unfortunately, they have standardized the customer. Although some standardization is useful (e.g., market segmentation), it can be overused or misused.

In today's marketing world, product management has become product/customer management. The product audit (value assessment) must include the customer to the point where it equates the product and the customer as one total value. The goal here is to focus on the most valuable combination of products with customers. The customer profiles established in Unit 1 will act as your line of customers.

Instead of matching customers to your products, you need to match products to your customers. You want to increase the number of products to *current* customers as much as or more than products to *new* customers. The customer life cycle stages and the customer's multiple needs will drive the product's placement in the overall product line.

The Product Element

The product aspect of this audit centers around the item or service you are marketing to the customer. First you must establish what your current product offerings are and who are they targeting. You do this by determining why your products exist, whom they are designed for, and what their value is in terms of features and benefits. Make sure your products are meeting the customers' needs and that your customers are being managed as your product line is being managed. Are your products really meeting the needs of customers, or do they exist because your research and development department likes them? Product purpose and level of customer satisfaction should be determined for both past and present products.

Product Line Identification

You need to establish your products' purposes for the target market they address. As shown in Format 47, this includes evaluating past products that have been discontinued to determine why they failed or their value was exhausted. Also evaluate your current product offerings and what their expected actions are.

Format 47

Product Purpose

Past Products (Have been discontinued over the last three years. Ranked by order of product/market introduction date.)

Product	Purpose
Model XYZ	Works on removing stains from clothing
Model XY2	Works on clothing to protect from stains

Present Products (Existing products for sale for the next three years. Ranked by order of product/market introduction date.)

Product	Purpose

As marketers, we are not concerned with the technical specifications of a product or service. We want to know how the technical components, formulas, or structure translate into financial gain and performance. If the product or service in question is not for profit, how does it help people? Although technical specifications are important (especially if the substance is proprietary), how customers accept and think of a product or service is more important.

Customer Line Identification

Every product needs to serve a customer. This exercise identifies the specific customer your products are targeted for. Your objective is to assign every product you are marketing to a customer based on the customer's desire to purchase your product.

When you are defining your customer, keep in mind you can have several customer profiles for each product. You may have a customer who acts as the buyer, but the end user may be someone totally different (e.g., a parent buys for a child). Use Format 48 to identify your target market(s) based on customer profiles. Because of space limitations, these sample descriptions are a little broad. You may need to be more specific by using age, income level, etc., to define your customer.

Format 48

Target Markets

Past Products (Have been discontinued over the last three years. Ranked by order of product/market introduction date.)

Product	Customer/Target Market(s)
Model XYZ	Women who work and run a household in the United States
Model XY2	Women and men who don't have time to spend cleaning a house in the United States

Present Products (Existing products for sale for the next three years. Ranked by order of product/market introduction date.)

Product	Customer/Target Market(s)

You can enter the data in these formats based either on your point of view or on the customer's. Although ideally they need to be the same, the key is to balance the customer's view with your company's view—the customer is not always right, but his or her opinion counts. To help you understand the relationship between product and customer, and how this relationship turns into opportunity and therefore value, Exhibit 2-1 isolates where your best business potential is or could be.

The final part of defining your products is establishing the distinctive factors that make your products better than the alternatives. Very few products can just exist—they must meet a specific need. Even products that claim to be multipurpose still offer something they believe to be unique. Use Format 49 to define your products by the distinctiveness of their qualities.

Exhibit 2-1				
Product/Market/Customer Opportunity Selection				
	Existing Customer Types	New Customer Types	Existing Geographic Markets	New Geographic Markets
Existing Products				
New Products				

Format 49

Distinctive Product Factors

Past Products (Have been discontinued over the last three years. Ranked in order of importance.)

Product	Distinctive Factors
Model ABC	*Worked in seconds—failed because of price.*
Model ABC2	*No mess of other liquids needed—failed because of competition.*

Present Products (Existing products for sale for the next three years. Ranked in order of importance.)

Product	Distinctive Factors

Portfolio and Life Cycle Management

Once you have identified your products and customers, you can begin to assess the real worth of the engine that produces your business income. The first step in this process is to outline your products' features and corresponding benefits in order to establish why they are and will be successful. Keep the target market in mind, and make sure you are satisfying the customers' needs or solving their problems.

Product Features

A *feature* is an attribute that represents a product's ability to perform the task for which it was designed. In establishing your product's features, you may find it valuable to break them down into primary and secondary classifications. For example, if you are marketing electronic items such as videotape players for the home, your products might have hundreds of features, but if you are marketing a part for a product you might need only one or two features. What counts are the features that customers want when making a purchasing decision. In the videotape player example, search preview or advanced programming would be primary features.

Product Benefits

Each feature a product possesses should have a corresponding benefit. A *benefit* is the value a customer places on a function or the feeling the product produces through its features. You'll need to cite your product research data to determine how customers view the specific benefits of your product. Just as with features, benefits can be classified into primary and secondary levels of importance. This information will be key in later product marketing planning activities such as branding and packaging.

Use Format 50 to tally your products' features and benefits.

Format 50		
Product Features and Benefits		
Product	Features	Benefits
Model XYZ	All controls are placed on one remote control	Easy to use
Model XY2	Two-step programming system	User-friendly when selecting programs

Product Identity

In the consumer package product and service industries, a product's features and benefits are not enough; its brand identity is the crucial component. Depending on the product, the appeal many times is not only what the product can do, but what it looks like. You can determine how effective your product's branding has been by analyzing image and appearance.

Image deals with the message the actual product is conveying, and appearance deals with how the product is contained for sale. Many elements drive a customer to make a purchase. You must establish what image your product has been projecting and what the results have been in terms of sales. The image a product projects drives the product's brand identity. Image is defined as what the brand represents. This means that when a product's brand is being formed, the message or symbol you're trying to convey to a customer through the name, flavor, or theme identifies the product. Use Format 51 to record your product's brand identity on the basis of product image.

Format 51

Product Image

| Product | Image | |
	Brand Name	Brand Theme
Model XYZ	Fast Start	All in one
Model XY2	Fun House	So advanced it's simple

In the industrial manufacturing/business-to-business world, product imaging is still important, but it focuses on functionality. Labeling and packaging still play a role, but they are limited to addressing proper operations or installation. The imaging role in this sector centers around quality, reliability, availability, service/support, cost, and improved performance. Image still plays a major role in establishing product value.

Appearance is defined as the physical product itself and/or the package (if needed) in which that product is sold. In the consumer package product and service industries, appearance is vital at the point of sale because it determines how your product is perceived by the customer when it is sitting on a shelf.

Judgments of appearance can be based on substance, shape, color, size, labeling, or protective packaging. The key is getting the customer to act based on his or her perception of the product's appearance. Whether the perceived quality is real or imagined is not the issue—the customer's perception is the issue. Ask yourself the following questions regarding the brand appearance of your product:

- Does the package serve a useful purpose? Does it protect the product?

- Does the package communicate what your product/brand does or is?

- Does the product demonstrate a sellable and valuable attribute?

Use Format 52 to evaluate your brand appearance.

		Format 52	

Product Appearance

		Product Appearance	
Product	Brand Name	Actual (by itself)	Package (as sold)
Model XYZ	Fast Start	Black and silver, designed for a human hand	Clear plastic package with bold futuristic lettering
Model XY2	Fun House	Small and compact in stylish white case with bright electronic LCD lights	(Product unseen) Protective white carton with clearly marked instructions

In the industrial manufacturing/business-to-business industries, appearance is far less important, and packaging is meant to be functional, not to stimulate sales. Appearance can be a consideration, but it is truly based on the specific product and its application.

Product Life Cycle Review

To this point, the definition of a life cycle was confined to the customer and the market. Products also have a life cycle that can drive their marketability. The customer's life cycle is based on life-changing events, whereas the product's life cycle (like that of a market) is based on life (introduction) to death (termination) actions. Management of product, market, and customer life cycles can point to market opportunities. They can provide standards to help anticipate purchasing and production patterns and, therefore, establish sales value.

Products pass through four stages:

• introduction

• growth

• maturity

• decline

As a general rule, if you have a new product that is experiencing low sales, you can consider that stage the introduction. Any sales increase that is sustained for a period of six or more months signals the growth stage. When sales begin to slow, but stay steady and strong, your product has entered its maturity phase. Finally, when sales begin to decline and eventually drop off (over a six-month period), your product value is declining.

In assessing the value of a product, you need to establish not only the stage a product is at, as well as market factors, such as saturation point, but factors that affect your product's level of success. In short, what might cause those life cycle stages to stretch or shrink in time and move a product from one stage to another?

It is helpful to overlay the market life cycle against the product life cycle to compare how well your stages match up. For example, if your product is growing, but your target market is declining, something needs to be changed. Again, the goal is to:

- Establish where your products fall in their life cycle.

- Match those life cycles to your customer's and market's life cycles.

- Address the common characteristics in these life cycles to determine what you can expect in terms of sales and costs to produce those sales.

For example, if your product is using old technology or is dependent upon a small customer base, its value may be in question even though sales are strong. Therefore, marketing tactics would be needed to enhance or terminate that product's market presence. (See Format 53.)

Format 53

Product Life Cycle Stage

20___

Product	Customer	Product Life Cycle Stage	Customer Life Cycle Stage	Time	Factor
Model XYZ	Profile A	Maturity	Retirement	2 years	New competition
Model XY2	Profile B	Growth	New birth	1 year	Increased demand by customers

Establishing a product's life cycle stage affects the entire marketing process. An explanation of what marketing strategies to use during each stage of the product life cycle may be found in *Marketing Management*, 6th Edition, (New York: Prentice-Hall, 1988).

Evaluating the Product Mix

Probably your most important activity is to establish your current product portfolio. Where your products are positioned in your product line mix and how they are positioned against your competition can determine the direction of your subsequent marketing efforts. Your products are your company's wealth-building assets. The value of these assets is partly determined by what they offer the customer that is different from other product purchasing options.

By looking at your product mix, you can measure the products' levels of performance (sales, financial, quality, etc.) and evaluate how they compare with one another. You can then determine if your product line needs any modifications, additions, or deletions. It is important to link a product's growth and market share performance with its ability to contribute sales. You will perform this part of the exercise while establishing your product portfolio. Its purpose is to identify an actual sales volume percentage. This will allow you to cross-reference market share and growth rate with sales volume. Such an analysis will account for products that may be low sales volume performers but that still have value such as creating awareness of the remainder of your product line.

There are various ways to establish the value and future opportunities of your product mix or line. One exercise uses perceptual mapping to demonstrate how your products rate or rank as a group and individually. The portfolio model method used most often is based on your products' growth and market share resulting from sales volume. The model used most frequently to test portfolio validity is the Boston Consulting Group's Portfolio Analysis Matrix. This model evaluates each product and places a value on each one using the following categories:

- problem children—unpredictable, high-maintenance products (high growth/low market share; low income generators)

- stars—low-risk, high-return products (high growth/low market share; high income generators)

- dogs—high-risk, low-profit products (low growth/low market share; low income generators)

- cash cows—mature, solid-return, low-maintenance products (low growth/high market share; high income generators)

Like the product life cycle stages, your product portfolio model will help you identify what your products represent. Your goal is to assess how each product works with your other products from year to year and to determine each product's value in your product line.

Market share is based on the competition's sales and the market potential. However, you need to note not only your relative market share, but what is acceptable for your industry. Each product is identified by a letter at the point where market share and growth rate intersect. Use the model in Format 54 to note a product's activity for the last three and the next three years.

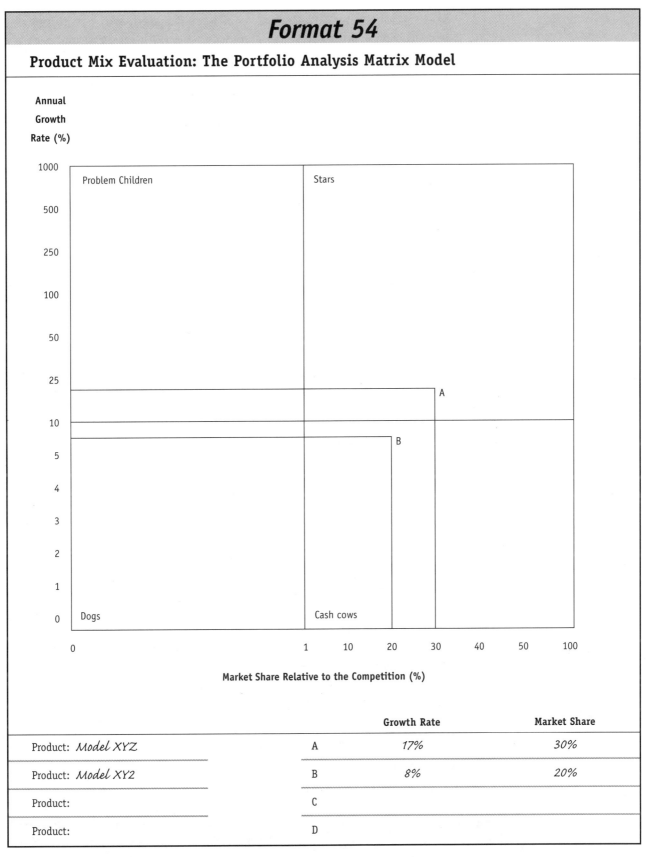

Format 54

Product Mix Evaluation: The Portfolio Analysis Matrix Model

Annual
Growth
Rate (%)

Problem Children   Stars

A

B

Dogs   Cash cows

Market Share Relative to the Competition (%)

		Growth Rate	Market Share
Product: *Model XYZ*	A	*17%*	*30%*
Product: *Model XY2*	B	*8%*	*20%*
Product:	C		
Product:	D		

Source: The Boston Consulting Group, Inc.

The Boston Consulting Group model has been the standard, but it does not relate well to customer impact on the product mix, and it tends to inaccurately portray fast-changing markets and product-to-market dynamics. Consider looking at other methods to establish the strengths and weaknesses/high to low value of the products you offer to your customers. A life cycle matrix that references product performance indicators such as growth, profitability, and market share to customer performance indicators such as profitability, activity, volume/frequency and purchasing might be better suited to your business world.

Format 55 provides an example of how one might address life cycles of products, customers, and markets using a performance rating system. It looks at market types and the customers in those markets (by profile ID) and contrasts them to product types. In this example, you are attempting to isolate the life cycle stage that is the most attractive and the points at which you can expect the best and worst performances. You can alter this life cycle stage to stages you select (i.e., introduction, growth, maturity, and decline) if you prefer. Format 55 simply offers one viewpoint from which to review how you use life cycle management in your marketing practices.

Determining Your Products' Sales Contribution

Another method of determining your products' value to your product line is to assess their financial contribution. This is an excellent way to compare your products' performance; however, you must keep in mind each product's overall impact. One product, for example, might have a low sales volume with a low profit margin, but it might be recession-proof or lead a customer to purchase other products. These are qualities that must be considered when evaluating a product's value.

Format 56 allows you to view each of your product's financial impact compared to your overall product line and compared to the customers who will buy it. First identify each product. Using your past sales reports, take each sales amount and divide it into the entire product lines' sales. Your total should equal 100 percent. In addition to each product's sales percentage, record your gross profit margin (in percentage) for each product. The goal is to see which products and customers are contributing the most to your business from a sales growth and profitability perspective. The better the return, the more valuable your product/customer mix can be.

New Product Impact

The product audit addresses your current performance, with support in some cases from previous and future (expected) performances. Your audit should also identify product opportunities. These can arise from changes, replacements, or additions to current products. New product development plans will be discussed later in this unit. The key for now is to acknowledge that new products—and the

Format 55

Life Cycle Management

Product Category: Brand X

		New Sale			Accessory Sale			Resale			New Additional Sale		
		Profitability	Activity	Frequency	Profitability	Activity	Frequency	Profitability	Activity	Frequency	Profitability	Activity	Frequency
Market Segment	Target market A	1	2	1	2	2	1	1	1	2	1	1	1
Customer Profile	Good customer	1	1	1	4	3	2	1	2	1	4	2	2
Customer Profile	Poor customer	4	2	3	3	2	3	4	1	2	3	4	3

Product Category: Brand XXX

		New Sale			Accessory Sale			Resale			New Additional Sale		
		Profitability	Activity	Frequency	Profitability	Activity	Frequency	Profitability	Activity	Frequency	Profitability	Activity	Frequency
Market Segment	Target market B	2	1	2	1	1	2	2	2	1	2	2	2
Customer Profile	Happy customer	2	3	2	2	1	4	3	4	3	2	3	1
Customer Profile	Bad customer	3	4	4	1	4	1	2	3	4	1	1	4

Performance Rating:
1 Best
2
3
4
5
6
7
8
9
10 Worst

Format 56

Sales Contribution

Product/Customer	Percentages of Sales	Gross Profit Margin
Model XYZ1	50%	50%
Customer Profile A	50%	40%
Customer Profile B	50%	20%
Customer Profile C	100%	30%
Model XYZ2	50%	50%
Customer Profile A	50%	40%
Customer Profile B	50%	20%
Total Products	100%	50%
Total Customer Profile A	100%	40%
Total Customer Profile B	100%	20%
Total Customer Profile C	100%	30%
Total Customers	100%	30%

Total customers must be calculated separately to arrive a a 100% level of contribution and the total gross profit margin (GPM will be shown as an average or weighted average).

new customers they will attract—can be pivotal in assessing your product performance. As Exhibit 2-1 indicated, the mixture of new/current products and new/current customers can allow you to create strong marketing strategies and tactics. Again, the key is to uncover where new developments could enhance your product value and add exciting business possibilities to your total product mix.

In identifying new product ideas, follow the same exercises you used with your current products. You'll need to establish the target market, the features/ benefits/incentives, competitive advantages, and product imaging suggested to validate these new product ideas.

In the final analysis, your products, income sources, and the customers to whom you are marketing must translate into a dollar value. Think of these elements as assets, and try to determine their worth and impact on your company. Yes, there are situations where non-dollar generation has value and should be noted, but the main thrust in assessing your products, income, and customers is establishing how this mix can best perform. The result will indicate which elements need to be replaced, added, or altered to create the best business potential.

Sales Performance Evaluation

The next step in assessing the value of your products is to analyze their sales volume. With these exercises, you are attempting to establish the track record of your products. Sales alone will provide only part of the story (good or bad) because the factors that generate sales volume can be influenced by uncontrollable circumstances. Nonetheless, sales performance can provide a solid indicator to a product's real worth as long as performance numbers are qualified and supported by other key financial data.

Historical Sales

As shown in Formats 57 to 60, you should always track your sales by product, customer type, geographic area, and store outlet (if it is a consumer package product or service industry) or distributor (if it is an industrial manufacturing/business to business industry). Track sales levels by units and by dollar amounts, showing growth rates as well. If you have products that are new to the marketplace, sales will have to be predicted.

Although it is valuable to look at sales records from as far back as possible, sales records from the past three years will give you the best indication of future sales. Growth rates are figured in units. Total growth rates are shown as an average.

Format 57

Sales by Product

Product(s)	19__			19__			19__		
	$	Units	%	$	Units	%	$	Units	%
Model XYZ	$10,000	1,000	—	$11,000	1,500	50	$13,900	1,700	13
Model XY2	8,700	886	—	10,500	1,000	13	12,000	1,200	20
Total									

Format 58

Sales by Customer Type

Product: XYZ

Customer Type	$	19___ Units	%	$	19___ Units	%	$	19___ Units	%

Format 59

Sales by Geographic Area

Product: XYZ

Geographic Area	$	19___ Units	%	$	19___ Units	%	$	19___ Units	%

Format 60

Sales by Store Outlet or Distributor

Product: XYZ

Distribution Channel	$	19__ Units	%	$	19__ Units	%	$	19__ Units	%

Forecasted Product Sales

Formats 61 to 64 provide a framework for forecasting sales for the current year and the next two years. The formats provided are identical to those for historical sales.

Format 61

Forecasted Sales by Product

Product	$	20__ Units	%	$	20__ Units	%	$	20__ Units	%
Total									

Format 62

Forecasted Sales by Customer Type

Product: XYZ

Customer Type	$	20__ Units	%	$	20__ Units	%	$	20__ Units	%
Total									

Format 63

Forecasted Sales by Geographic Area

Product: XYZ

Geographic Area	$	20__ Units	%	$	20__ Units	%	$	20__ Units	%
Total									

Format 64									
Forecasted Sales by Store Outlet or Distributor									
Product: *XYZ*									
Distribution Channel	$	20__ Units	%	$	20__ Units	%	$	20__ Units	%
Total									

Estimating New Product Sales

If you have a new product that will appear in the market in the next three years, you'll have no historical sales data from which to forecast sales. You will need to estimate sales volume in other ways. Estimating is different from forecasting. Estimating means what you hope may happen, while forecasting means what you believe will happen. The difference is small but important in estimating a new product's sales performance.

Use Formats 65 to 68 to determine what sales will be for your new products and to examine the impact of new products on current sales forecasts. To obtain these data, use your own product research and historical sales performance of similar products. This information, along with current sales forecasts, will allow you to estimate sales of new products. The formats allow you to predict your sales information based on product, customer type, geographic area, and store outlet or distributor.

Analyzing Product Sales Patterns

Raw sales volume results are one way of assessing your performance levels. Another method is to identify patterns, changes, and fluctuation in those sales volumes. In short, you're addressing how and why those results were produced. This helps you determine whether or not your sales run in cycles so that you can forecast sales more accurately. It also helps you plan production, inventory, and raw material purchases.

Format 65

Estimated New Product Sales

Product	$	20__ Units	%	$	20__ Units	%	$	20__ Units	%
Total									

Format 66

Estimated New Product Sales by Customer Type

Product: XYZ

Customer Type	$	20__ Units	%	$	20__ Units	%	$	20__ Units	%
Total									

Format 67

Estimated New Product Sales by Geographic Area

Product: *XYZ*

Geographic Area	$	20__ Units	%	$	20__ Units	%	$	20__ Units	%
Total									

Format 68

Estimated New Product Sales by Store Outlet or Distributor

Product: *XYZ*

Store Outlet	$	20__ Units	%	$	20__ Units	%	$	20__ Units	%
Total									

Identifying Sales Trends

The first objective is to identify whether or not your sales patterns reflect any continual change or trend. A trend is a consistent change in sales in any direction with any volume. If the trend holds for more than three years, it may be considered a permanent pattern in your sales activity.

Format 69 gives you a way to see how specific trends can have an impact on your product's sales, positively or negatively. First identify each product and list trends that could affect it; then link that effect with its impact on your product. For example, let's say your product meets a specific customer need to rent videotapes of movies. A trend that could affect that need would be development of a new technology such as video CDs or a new service such as pay-per-view cable TV.

Format 69		
Product Sales Trends		
Product	**Trend**	**Impact**
Model XYZ	Use of CD technology	Must replace product soon
Model XY2	Customers wanting pay-per-view	Product losing value (sales), must change

Seasonal Fluctuations in Sales

Sales changes that are the same year after year are considered to be cyclical or seasonal. This means that, for whatever reason, sales will move in the same direction with the same degree of impact each year. Your sales forecast can be adjusted to anticipate the seasonal changes.

Use Format 70 to track sales fluctuations by placing a point at the appropriate unit sales levels under each month and connecting the points with a line. Remember, you will need to complete this chart for each of your products. Besides identifying product sales changes, this format allows you to overlay market sales for comparison purposes. Again, track market sales by placing a point at the appropriate unit levels and then connecting the points to form a line. The sample format here is based on unit sales of one to ten. Depending upon your sales volume, you may need to adjust the scale to hundreds or even thousands of units.

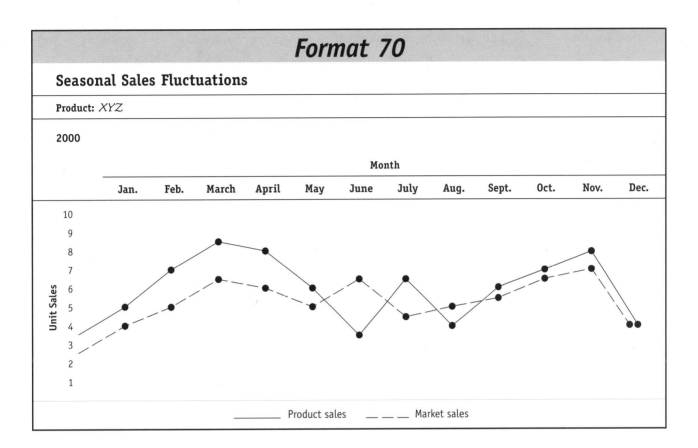

Financial Profitability Measurement

The center of the marketing universe is profitability. Yes, sales and market share are important, but the ability to generate a profit is even more important. Product pricing and costing standards will go a long way in determining the value of the products you are marketing. Establishing how much money you can generate from a single product unit sale is crucial. As a marketer, it is important that you know your products' roles in your company's financial well-being. Work closely with your controller or accountant to ensure that your calculations are accurate.

Establishing Product Price/Cost Structure

The first step in establishing the profitability of your product line is to develop your product price/cost structure. To do this, you must define your base price, special allowances such as volume discounts, and cost of goods sold. Then you will be able to establish your gross revenue, profit margin, and profit levels. In determining your cost of goods sold, work with your accounting department to select an appropriate cost formula. The formula should include:

- cost and sales volume relationships

- extent of control over costs

In determining your pricing policies, again work with your accounting department to evaluate the price formula to be used, which should include:

- impact of product management and distribution tactics

- impact of costs, competition, and legal variables

- impact of price on customers and on your overall marketing strategies

Your accounting and finance departments, production, engineering, and legal counsel should participate in assessing current and future pricing practices.

Format 71 allows you to establish your price/cost and profit structure. To use this format you must identify each product and establish the discount structure for the products. In this case, we will use volume discounting. Begin by counting the first unit; then break down your discount structure into any increments. (The examples shown are in increments from 1–9, 10–19, and 20–50.) Finally, place your products' prices in the format.

The discount variable can be used in place of or along with the variable known as allowances. This variable can be included to account for losses, returns, or damage. By adding allowances to your calculations you can quantify the amount of financial risk associated with a product sale based on customer, market, marketing mix, or product tendencies.

The remainder of the format is based on simple calculations. Subtract the dollar amount of each volume discount from your base price. (Remember that the first increment will have a discount of $0.) Then subtract the discount from the price base to find your revenue. Insert the cost of goods sold in the next line on the chart and then subtract your cost of goods sold from the revenue level to determine gross profit. Finally, convert the profit level into a percentage by taking the gross profit in dollars and dividing by revenue.

Format 71

Product Price/Cost Structure

Product: XYZ				Product: XY2
Volume (units)	(1–9)	(10–19)	(20–50)	(1 – +)
Price ($)	689	689	689	1,089
Allowance ($)	0	50	100	0
Revenue ($)	689	639	589	1,089
Cost of goods sold ($)	260	260	260	520
Gross profit ($)	$429	$379	$329	$569
Gross margin (%)	62%	59%	56%	52%

There are no general rules to determine if your profit margin is favorable. You will need to evaluate the final percentages based on industry standards and company goals. However, if your gross profit is very low—10 percent or less— you may want to reconsider the product's feasibility.

You may also want to look at your price/cost structure as it relates to customer type. Customer profitability is just as important as product profitability. Customer profitability is addressing all the direct costs associated with reaching, securing, and maintaining a customer. This will include cost of goods sold, as well as the cost of marketing. The pricing aspect, along with these costs, can provide an additional viewpoint from which to assess your product's true level of profitability.

Cost of goods sold, which is defined as the direct materials or resources needed to create a product or service, may need to be modified for your own business. For example, if you are a financial lender, costs of funds may be the appropriate costing variable to use.

Analyzing Product Profit Structure

After you have established your per-unit price/cost structure, your next objective is to set up a profit structure. You do this by combining the historical sales patterns for the last three years with your present price/cost structure to determine how much gross income can be produced. This information will reflect the strengths and weaknesses in your products' revenues and help you establish a product's value to the product line.

Format 72 allows you to combine your pricing structure with your past sales reports and your present sales forecasts to calculate your revenue stream. Your source for sales volumes and growth rates is sales reporting and forecasting information. Your pricing structure will provide information on cost of goods sold, gross profit, and gross margins. Multiply your pricing data by your unit sales to determine your profit structure.

Format 72			
Product Profit Structure ($ thousands)			
Product: *XYZ*	20__	20__	20__
Sales ($)	*475,785*	*626,565*	*758,367*
Sales (units)	*740*	*975*	*1,180*
Growth (%)	*N/A*	*32*	*21*
Cost of goods sold ($)	*209,300*	*303,160*	*404,042*
Gross profit ($)	*$266,485*	*$323,405*	*$354,325*
Gross margin (%)	*56%*	*52%*	*47%*

When analyzing your profit structure, you need to answer the following questions:

- Will customers accept a price that covers your cost of goods?

- Is growth of sales outpacing increases in costs?

- Is there ample gross margin? (Depending on the industry standard, you need to have a strong gross margin to compensate for your net margins to be able to generate suitable profit levels. Work with your controller or accountant to determine an acceptable gross margin.)

- Are you making money?

- At what point in sales volume do you break even or do your total costs begin to drop off? What are the revenue implications of this break-even point? (Again, you will need to work with your financial department to perform a break-even analysis and to understand the total revenue picture.) The break-even point will tell you when your sales start to represent true returns and how long it will take for the product to pay itself off.

- How does lower or higher pricing increase sales volume? Do more sales of current products, the addition of new products, or the raising or lowering of costs impact profit performance? (Remember that when adding new products, sales will not always be a total gain because the new products will probably take away from sales of current products.)

Determining Financial Return

After reviewing your product's ability to produce a profit, you need to address the key financial measurements of that profit. The financial performance of a product as it relates to resources consumed can tell you the return your product is producing. Meet with your finance and accounting people to select the proper financial return calculation process.

To understand the financial return of a product, you need to separate your products into two categories: current products and new products being developed or under consideration.

A current product's return is a relatively simple calculation to make because you are measuring the pure performance of annual investment dollars (assets or equity), minus any additional research and development payback, against the income generated. Your rate of return, or return on investment, is shown as the percentage earned in comparison to the percentage of dollars spent.

A new product's return is more difficult to calculate because you are taking into account the cost to produce a product over an extended time period. Your analysis also needs to address time as it relates to the research and development payback and realized income (income over and above cost). Because the product is new, no historical records of performance exist, so estimating the uncertain future of earnings potential is risky. When a product is being considered for a market, the questions are: Is it worth the risk? How much money will I have to spend to make money? When can I expect to realize this income?

Use the following key indicators to measure financial return by product and overall product line:

- return on investment (ROI)

- discounted cash flow

- payback period

- break-even analysis (units and dollars)

These indicators (separately or together) can help you measure the return you are receiving or can expect. You can verify how changes to your products or marketing tactics are affecting your products' financial return.

Besides ROI, you can also look at ROA (return on assets) and ROE (return on equity). For purposes of product profitability in the world of the marketer, ROI is usually the better indicator to cite. You will also need to determine the baseline number or data point from which your product's financial performance will be measured. This data point can come from one or all of the following sources:

- historical company records

- industry standards (found in Unit 1, "Identification of Marketing Industry Standards")

- published industry standards (e.g., Robert Morris Associates)

These sources act as a benchmark from which to compare yourself. If you are higher or lower than the standards, you can determine how valuable your products are and what changes may be needed to improve or maintain performance levels.

Your audit findings should indicate how you calculate financial return by product and overall product line. By including the current and projected return expected from current and new products under development you can decide if your current measurements, standards, and logic provide the accurate financial return data you need to make the appropriate decisions. Thus, you can determine if the financial return you are experiencing is adequate or if changes need to be made.

Production Capacity Determination

However great the demand for your products is, if you can't fill orders, your customers will be disappointed. You must determine your ability to produce a product that fits your financial resources and can adjust to customer sales cycles. If yours is a service-based company, you must address your ability to serve customers. In this environment, production takes on a different meaning, but the bottom line is to meet customer purchase demands.

Establishing Your Production Capabilities

The first step in measuring your production capabilities is to establish your maximum production levels. Determine your comfortable production ranges and consider when you might need to enlarge your space, increase your machinery, add suppliers, or hire more workers. Then be prepared to adjust your cost structuring as required by these changes.

Format 73 provides a method of establishing your production activity levels. By calculating how many workers it takes to make your products, and various ranges of production speed, you can assess your ability to adjust and predict production strengths and weaknesses. These factors, combined with machinery and raw material supply, will help define what production capacity you can support. You may want to reconfigure the format to accommodate your product line as a whole.

Production capacity is one of the factors you will use in determining your sales forecasts, so, you need to plan realistic production levels.

Format 73

Production Capacity

Year	Product	No. of Employees	Size of Facility	Production Volume Levels Low	Medium	Maximum
20___	A	22	Entire plant (100 sq. ft.)	1,000	1,500	2,000
20___	B	25	Entire plant (100 sq. ft.)	1,200	1,700	2,200
20___	C	25	Plant expand (150 sq. ft.)	1,300	1,800	2,300

Determining Your Production Resources and Limitations

It's important to know the limits of your current production operations and at what point you will change them; planned changes must be compatible with future sales activities. You also need to indicate if any changes such as new investments or changes in production costs are anticipated in your internal or external resources. What impact will these changes have on production?

In analyzing the capacity of your internal production operations, be sure to include your manufacturing plant and production workers, and base your assessment on your present and future needs. Use the three factors provided in Format 74-1. This information will make you aware of your situation and what steps (if any) you may need to take to prepare for the future.

Format 74-1

Production Resources and Limitations

	Present Status	Future Plans
Production facilities	Small assembly area	New assembly area purchase for expansion (two years out)
Work force	Medium skilled	New education program to improve skill levels (next year)
Machinery	Old mechanical equipment	New computerized equipment (within the year)

Use Format 74-2 to establish the capacity of your external production operations. This analysis includes independent production subcontractors and their workers and is based on your present and future needs.

Format 74-2

Production Resources and Limitations

	Present Status	Future Plans
Outside supplement		
Production facilities		

Evaluating Operational Control

In this section, you are primarily concerned with events and actions that affect your production and delivery capabilities. You must identify present and alternative sources of supplies, problems that affect product delivery and material availability, and areas in which you have competitive advantages.

Use Formats 75-1 and 75-2 to define your delivery and supplier selections. This exercise will help you understand who is delivering your product to the customer and who is providing you with the material for manufacturing. This information will give you a good basis for making decision about these processes.

Product Delivery

The delivery of your product to your customers on time and undamaged is crucial. Delivery is the link between your production lines and fulfillment of the sales order. Whether you perform this task internally or externally, you should establish present and future sources of delivery. Use Format 75-1 as a guideline.

Format 75-1

Operational Control

Source	Present Status	Future Plans
In-house	Using for 90% of all deliveries	No change
Independent	Using only for overflow	No change

Materials Suppliers

The suppliers of the materials, parts, and components that comprise your product are also vital. Try to build relationships with suppliers who can provide quality materials when they are needed. Use Format 75-2 to analyze your present and future sources of materials. You should also weigh the importance of each supplier to your operations, considering lead time requirements, risk of shortages, and terms of contracts.

Format 75-2

Operational Control

Source	Present Status	Future Plans
In-house	Have exclusive contracts	Will branch out to have alternatives
Independent	Using only when needed	Will open up for bids

Assessing Competitive Operating Advantages and Disadvantages

Summarize the competitive advantages in your overall operational control, taking into account production capacity, delivery of product, suppliers' ability to meet your needs, proprietary techniques, level of experience, and lower costs. These strengths can later translate into marketing strategies.

Likewise, disadvantages need to be identified to expose where problems may occur in contrast to your competitors. Production weaknesses need to be dealt with just as production strengths are.

Legal Concerns

You must not undertake any marketing activity that is in violation of current or pending laws. Your objective is to identify legal issues that may be confronting your product's entry into the marketplace. You must protect yourself from lawsuits by those who may claim you have stolen their ideas and prevent others from stealing your ideas so you will not have to take legal action. Legal actions can decrease the financial value of your company and your products.

Evaluating Your Product's Legal Control

The protection of copyrights, patents, trade secrets, and trademarks as they relate to a product's integrity is paramount, so make sure you apply for the appropriate legal protection and use any legally required labeling for your products. Although some products can't be protected, most can be to some degree.

Use Format 76 to record the status of any legal efforts that are being undertaken on behalf of your product(s). The sample pertains to the status of patent filing procedures for two different models of a product.

Format 76		
Legal Control		
Product	Filing Status	Date Fully Covered
Model XYZ	Phase 1 filing (patent pending)	Next year—June 1
Model XY2	Not patentable	Not available

Assessing Product Liability

In this day of personal injury litigation, you need to determine your degree of exposure to product liability. If you are liable for damages caused by your product, you have to measure your level of risk and perhaps obtain liability insurance. If you do buy insurance, its cost should be integrated into your general expenses.

Format 77 offers a method of evaluating your liability exposure. This exercise helps you gauge the likelihood that your product could create an unfair or unsafe situation due to negligence in its creation, design, or use. This determination should come from your attorney. You then need to discuss the steps you would take to protect yourself from the legal consequences of this negligence. This could involve product liability insurance, labeling awareness, liability releases, legal positioning, or nothing. Doing nothing is not as bad as it sounds. You must meet the rules governing your product's existence, and it must perform fairly and safely, within reason. However, many times companies feel that it is cheaper to fight or settle lawsuits than to take on the cost of preventing problems from arising.

Format 77

Product Liability

Product	Level of Exposure	Cost of Insurance
Model XYZ	Very small	No insurance
Model XY2	Medium to high	Heavy insurance $1,000,000 coverage $20,000 cost per year

Product liability costs are key, and it is marketing's role to provide this information to the accountant or controller who is figuring the product's financials.

Examining Outstanding Contracts and Agreements

Another legal matter to consider is outstanding contracts with vendors, suppliers, distributors, salespeople, competitors, and current or former employees. Contracts are designed to protect an individual's rights; you need to make sure that your marketing activities don't violate these contracts.

Use Format 78 to track legal issues that could affect your marketing program. For each product, determine what legal issues, if any, are pending. This analysis will help you see if you need outside funding or if there is a legal problem that could delay or halt a product's manufacturing.

Format 78

Legal Agreements

Product	Nondisclosure Agreements	Noncompete Agreements	Outstanding/Pending Product Litigation
Model XYZ	None	One—with former joint venture partner	None
Model XY2	None	None	Yes—former stock owner, for compensation

New Product Thinking and Planning Analysis

Up to this point, your product audit has focused on current product, customer, and income sources. These sources have been discussed only in terms of assessing how changes to the existing mix might be improved. If change mandates new product developments, a process must be in place to take a new concept from thought to reality. Use the guidelines in this section to assess if your product development process is meeting your needs.

Product innovation and creativity are the cornerstones of marketing. Very few markets can be serviced by a company that offers the same product year after year without enhancements, replacements, or additions. Therefore, your product audit should look at potential product ideas, addressing not only product possibilities, but also your ability to bring a product to market.

The following product development tactics could impact the value of current and new products:

- cost reductions

- product alterations (features)

- product elimination

- price changes

- product improvements

The following actions would result from those tactics:

- product refinements
- product additions
- product deletions
- product replacements

Products can be completely new products or reintroductions. Branding changes in the consumer package product and service industries would follow the same option structure as the product development process.

Assessing Past Product Developments

The objective in examining former products is to identify the status of products you have or have not added to your product line. You want to determine how successful you were at developing the product, how successful the product was once it was released, and whether the product met the expectations originally established. Format 79 provides space to list products under development. Be sure to list the date a product was released into the market and a performance rating of your choice. You may want to expand the results section of this format to include information such as the product's performance at the target market and prototype stages.

Format 79

Products Under Development

Product	Purpose	Target Market	Results
Model 123 Cleaner	Home cleaner	Women 30–40 yrs.	Released 6-30-99— very successful
Model 321 Cleaner	Auto cleaner	Men 20–30 yrs.	terminated— did not test well with market

Evaluating Product Development Status and Plans

Once you understand what you did in the past, you can determine the status of present product developments. Your objective is to find out where specific products are in the research and development stages. Project development stages include developing, assessing, designing, building, and testing product for market introduction.

A product is in constant motion. As you complete Format 80, your objective is to bring definition to a product's status and activity at a given stage. In determining the status of new products, remember to include not only products that exist in your own environment but also those you are acquiring through acquisition, merger, joint venture, or licensing arrangements with another party. The objective is to identify where you stand with products that may or may not be added to your existing product line.

Format 80

Product Development Status

Product Description	Stage	Purpose/Use	Target Market	Expected Release Date
Model 101	Concept	Home cleaning	Hispanic women	2-00
Model XXX	Product testing	Home repair	White men	1-01

Establishing Product Development Processes

Once you determine past and present product development activities, you can evaluate your research and testing procedures. To do this, you must consider various industries and business needs. Exhibit 2-2 offers four examples of processes various companies have used. The examples show varying degrees of detail but share a similar flow.

The initial stage in the product development process consists of creating a product idea and assessing its validity. Designing and building come next, followed by testing and measurement. Finally, the product is released, with customer feedback linked to the market introduction.

Whether your idea changes a current product or introduces a new entry, the process must be followed to ensure quality and performance. The key is to determine if your current process is adequate to produce quality new product ideas and if the ideas will meet the expectations originally established.

Exhibit 2-2

Product Development Process

Example A	Example B	Example C	Example D
1. Concept development	1. Idea formulation	1. Product proposal	1. Brain storming
2. Market, costing, and profitability assessment	2. Concept assessment	2. Market assessment	2. Technical feasibility
3. Design specifications	3. Submission and approval	3. Costing assessment	3. Legal confirmation
4. Development and building	4. Commencement	4. Profitability assessment	4. Market analysis
5. Marketing research, analysis, and planning	5. Design and development	5. Design and build specifications	5. Selling price estimation
6. Product testing	6. Building	6. Marketing management planning	6. Technical specifications
7. Product trials	7. Procedures development	7. Limited release	7. Customer impression
8. Product release	8. Testing	8. Field testing	8. Product analysis
9. Customer or channel satisfaction tracking	9. Modifications	9. Full release	9. Packaging development
	10. Implementation	10. Customer and sales feedback	10. Selling systems mechanism
	11. Closure and maintenance		11. Order processing management
			12. Legal arrangements—contracts
			13. Selling price development
			14. Product marketing plan—design
			15. Limited production
			16. Field performance testing
			17. Product marketing plan—implementation
			18. Mass production
			19. Support allocation—service activation
			20. Distribution—billing and shipping
			21. Customer feedback

The main areas a marketer must contend with are:

- Product research—a form of research conducted directly with the customer at various stages of the product's development. The purpose is to determine the customer's perception of the product, what needs the product must fill for the customer to purchase it, and how to make the customer a loyal customer.

- Performance testing—an actual physical test in which a product's features are evaluated, usually in a controlled, scientific setting. Testing can be conducted strictly as a function of the marketing department or as a combined effort between marketing research staffs and manufacturing/production.

- Market research—the process of identifying the areas into which a product will be sold. These areas (markets) are evaluated on criteria such as competition, size, legal regulations, and overall consumer purchasing patterns and acceptance.

- Marketing research—an umbrella term used to describe all research acts that fall under the business functions of marketing. More specifically, marketing research is used to define an ongoing research application (such as customer satisfaction) that is usually evaluated as part of an annual marketing plan.

Format 81 provides a method of establishing what testing and research activities are currently under way. This allows you to view various forms of testing in manufacturing and marketing environments and evaluate results.

Format 81

Product Testing

Product	Stage	Activities Conducted	Results
Model 990	Product testing	Product research/field customer acceptance	Modifications to target markets
Model 133	Product trials	Product research/customer brand awareness	Packaging changes

Service Support Assessment

For consumer package product and industrial manufacturing/business-to-business industries that market a physical product, the support or service aspect needs to be counted as part of the product's total value. In the world of value-added products, the service element can be an additional profit center or a cost center to serve other profit centers. This is key in this customer-driven marketing world. Customer service (type and performance) must be included.

To assess the service component, simply review how your support is rendered to the customer and determine how successful you have been at obtaining new customers, attracting former customers back, and maintaining current customers. The role of service will indicate not only current strengths and weaknesses, but also future opportunities and problems, based on your current customer management approach.

Unit 3

Evaluating the Effectiveness of Marketing Actions

Your audit so far covered how you approach and manage your marketplace. It established your income sources, and it assessed the performance or value of your products. Now you need to assess how effective you are at marketing your products. This unit will supply you with questions and exercises to consider in managing your marketing strategies and tactics.

The objective of this audit is to measure your ability as a company, or as a marketing area, to manage your marketing efforts and dollars. It takes you through the heart of marketing management, the *marketing mix*, which consists of nine marketing functions (advertising, sales, distribution, etc.) that drive the ability to reach, capture, and service customers. It offers ideas on the best methods of programming your marketing mix.

The Marketing Management Concept

The ultimate goal of these audits is to better understand the dynamics, issues, and drivers that cause your marketing efforts to succeed or fail. The final outcome is a marketing plan (strategic or tactical) that will act as your game plan to make more money or save more money than previous marketing efforts for the company. Marketing management centers on the relationship among strategy, tactics, and actions. The results of your audits will translate into your ability to capture business through the thoughts and activities you develop.

Marketing Overview

Strategy is the big-picture thinking of what you would like to accomplish and the impact it would have on your company. Historically, this was reflected as a long-term event, but into today's annual rate of return world, strategy is more "thinking out of the box" marketing. Formula-driven processes (tactics) are the action from which strategies are realized. Typically, a tactical plan is referred to as a marketing plan with an annual scope. Tactics are the tools available to market your products to your customers, against a predetermined performance goal. The action aspect of the plan includes the options available through those tactics. Actions are like push buttons on a computer—you program the buttons to produce the desired outcome.

Consumer package products, industrial manufacturing/business-to-business, and service industries all depend on solid marketing management to deliver on the marketing goals necessary to drive the company's ability to generate a profit. In all these industries, the customer is the key. Marketing is the ability to influence and direct the customer to purchase the products you have to offer.

Life cycle management of markets, customers, and products are all keys in predicting potential business opportunities. Market and product life cycles are based on the common stages of introduction, growth, maturity, and decline. When markets and products are entering, existing in, or leaving one of these stages, they experience common characteristics. These characteristics can tell you why a product may be performing lower or higher than expectations.

The customer life cycle, commonly referred to as *customer relationship marketing*, focuses on events an individual might experience in life and the relationship the person has with your products or company. By clarifying how marketing life cycles work, your audit findings will help you craft your ultimate analysis and planning efforts. As you audit the marketing management aspect of your business, the customer will be the centerpiece of your research. Stalking the modern customer, especially in the consumer package product and service industries, is getting more difficult every day. This audit will tell you how effective you have been at selling your products or services. In today's marketing world, customers must be managed just as products were in the past. Your audit findings should reflect the performance of marketing to customers versus marketing products to customers.

The first steps in auditing marketing management are in the area of performance reporting. This information will tell you how effective you have been at meeting your marketing goals, capturing customers, and producing product. These performances will be viewed by senior management, and they will want to know how you formed your beliefs and predictions regarding how you have been generating sales, obtaining profitability, and controlling your market position.

Marketing Performance Measurement

In marketing, sales and revenue are the number-one financial indicator of performance. This key measurement will tell you how effective (in terms of dollars generated) your marketing efforts have been to date. It profiles the sale of a product in volume and the consequential dollars produced.

Sales and Revenues Measurement

The first step in measuring sales and revenue is to define how your current sales forecasts are established; that is, what is the basis for these estimates? Then record your sales and revenue forecasts for the last three years and the next three years. Base your sales forecast on market potential, competition, production capacity, market trends, market financial health, your product's profitability, and your marketing activities and distribution processes. In evaluating your estimates, you should employ some verification measure to test the validity of the numbers. You must be as objective as possible in a subjective environment to ensure the accuracy of the estimates. Ask yourself the following questions:

Quantitative Verification

- Are your numbers time specific?

- Are your numbers measurable?

- Can you track your numbers by product, customer, sales, territory, and store outlet/distributor?

Qualitative Verification

- Are your numbers realistic?

- Are your numbers financially sound?

- Do the numbers reflect seasonal fluctuation?

Do your numbers stand up to these tests? Your answers should be challenging and attainable.

Forecasting Sales

In analyzing your current expected sales performance, you need to look at your sales from product and customer viewpoints. You should audit each product on its own merit, as well as the product line's total sales compared with your sales potential, to determine comfortable sales volume levels. Compare the actual sales with sales forecasts to see how accurately you predicted the future and how stable your sales volume has been.

Format 82 helps you evaluate how well you obtained your sales goals. You'll need to apply this format for the current and previous three-year time frames. Remember, your previous sales numbers are not a record of your actual sales; your analysis needs to reflect what you predicted sales would be compared to the actual sales.

Format 82

Sales Forecast ($ thousands)

	20__ $	20__ Units	20__ $	20__ Units	Rate of Growth (%)	20__ $	20__ Units	Rate of Growth (%)
Product: *Regular*	$405,000	675	$534,000	890	32	$646,200	1,077	21
Product: *Large*	70,785	65	92,565	85	32	112,167	103	21
Total	475,785	740	626,565	975	32	758,367	1,180	21

Measuring Sales Potential

The purpose of recording sales potential in Format 83 is to establish the maximum dollar or unit amount of product line your company is capable of supporting (selling, servicing, etc.). This is based primarily on your capability to produce and market (sell, distribute, and service customers) a product for a year. The purpose of recording a sales forecast is to predict estimated dollar or unit sales of your product line for the year. The sales forecast comes from the sales and revenue forecast you established in Format 82.

Format 83 allows you to compare your sales forecasts to your sales potential. Your objective is to determine how you formulate your sales potential and if it is accurately predicting your sales generation limitations.

To determine your percentage of growth, subtract the previous year's unit total from the following year's (i.e., subtract 2000 total from 1999 total); then

Format 83

Sales Forecast and Sales Potential ($ thousands)

	20__ $	20__ Units	20__ $	20__ Units	Rate of Growth (%)	20__ $	20__ Units	Rate of Growth (%)
Sales Potential								
Product: *Regular*	$605,000	1,008	$650,000	1,080	7	$700,000	1,165	8
Product: *Large*	80,000	75	100,000	90	20	150,000	140	56
Total	685,000	1,083	750,000	1,170	8	850,000	1,305	12
Sales Forecast								
Product: *Regular*	$405,000	675	$534,000	890	32	$646,200	1,077	21
Product: *Large*	70,785	65	92,565	85	32	112,167	103	21
Total	475,785	740	626,565	975	32	758,367	1,180	21

divide that amount by the previous year's total. This will establish a positive or negative growth rate. The total line at the bottom of the format represents average growth rates of the overall product line. Format 83 demonstrates a problem: your sales volume is outpacing your ability to handle these sales in your regular products and your overall product line.

Projecting Your Revenues

In order to define your current profitability projections, you need to calculate the revenues that will be generated by your sales forecasting. You are translating your sales expectations into earnings. Each year you need to make more money to cover rising costs or to reinvest in the company. You can do this by lowering costs, selling more products, or raising the product's price. Your product profitability statement will include product costs that are determined in the product development or product management section by your accountant or financial manager.

It's helpful to define your profitability projections by individual product and overall product line. Note that sales dollars are figured using the base unit price. If volume discount pricing is used your revenue figures may need to be adjusted. (See Format 84.)

Format 84

Revenue Projections ($ thousands)

Overall	20___	20___	20___
Sales ($)	475,785	626,526	758,367
Sales (units)	740	975	1,180
Rate of growth (%)	N/A	32	21
Cost of goods sold ($)	209,300	303,160	404,042
Gross profit ($)	$266,485	$323,366	$354,325
Gross margin (%)	56%	52%	47%

Market Share Movement

Market share measures your piece of the pie. This information helps you plan growth and gauge overall sales performance compared to the market and your competition. First you need to determine the basis for your market share estimates, which include the direction and speed of growth you will be experiencing in market share. Are you growing or declining, and at what speed? Once again, you need to demonstrate this by target market, overall product line, and individual product.

The following exercises present two ways to determine your perceived market share. Your goal is to establish a share level that reflects your presence in the marketplace. Remember that you are auditing what you believe to be your market share based on your sales performance. The market audit (Unit 1) is the official word on what your actual market share status really is. Determine what you believe to be your market share and compare that with market share audit information to accurately identify your market status.

Market Share Relative to the Market Potential

In establishing your current market share projections, you need to use two methods to analyze your market share. The first is by market share relative to the market itself. This can indicate your level of potential growth, which will come from obtaining a new portion of the market or from taking away part of a competitor's share. A good market share estimate relative to the market would be in the range of .05 to 1.00 percent.

Format 85 needs to be applied in a manner that reflects the last three and the next three years. This format helps you evaluate how effective you were at predicting your market share. The last three years are not a record of your actual market share reported; they show what you predicted your market share levels would be compared to what they actually were. Remember that market share is based on units, not sales. The next three years are used to verify your current market share predictions. They represent what you believe your market share levels will be, not actual market share obtained.

To complete Format 85 you will need to know your market potential. This information is located in Unit 1 under Market Size Determination. You can then divide your sales forecast by the market potential to arrive at your market share level, as shown in this sample calculation:

$$\frac{\text{Sales forecast: } 500 \text{ units}}{\text{Market potential: } 1,000,000 \text{ units}} = \text{Market share: } 0.05\%$$

The overall amounts on this format represent market share for the entire product line.

Market Share Relative to the Competition

The other commonly used method for assessing market share is rating your market share relative to the competition. This method is more popular simply because your numbers will appear larger. The problem with this method is that it does not tell you how much of the market is available for expansion. A typical

Format 85

Market Share Assessment Relative to the Market ($ thousands)

	20___ Units	Rate of Growth (%)	20___ Units	Rate of Growth (%)	20___ Units	Rate of Growth (%)
Market share (Units)						
Market share (Relative to market)						
Overall:	0.07	—	0.08	14	0.05	25
Product:	0.01	—	0.02	100	0.03	50
Product:	0.06	—	0.06	0	0.07	17

market share estimate (relative to the competition—direct, indirect, or alternatives) would be from 10 to 35 percent.

$$\frac{\text{Sales forecast:} \quad 500 \text{ units}}{\text{Market forecast:} \quad 100{,}000 \text{ units}} = \text{Market share: } 0.50\%$$

Format 86 also needs to reflect the last three and next three years. This exercise evaluates how well you predicted your market share. The last three years are not a record of your actual market share reported; they reflect what you predicted your market share levels would be compared to the actual levels. Remember, market share is based on units, not sales. The next three years verify your current market share predictions. They represent what you believe your market share levels will be, not actual market share obtained.

To complete Format 86 you need to know your market forecast. This information can be found in Unit 1 under Market Size Determination. An easy way to figure these data is to total all your sales and those of your competitors. Once you establish your sales forecast, divide that amount by your market forecast to arrive at your market share. Following is a sample calculation.

Format 86

Market Share Assessment Relative to the Competition ($ thousands)

	20___ Units	Rate of Growth (%)	20___ Units	Rate of Growth (%)	20___ Units	Rate of Growth (%)
Market share (Relative to competition)						
Overall:	30	—	35	17	40	14
Product:	20	—	20	0.00	25	25
Product:	10	—	15	50	15	0

$$\frac{\text{Sales forecast:} \quad 500 \text{ units}}{\text{Market forecast:} \quad 1,000 \text{ units}} = \text{Market share: } 50\%$$

The overall amounts on this format represent market share for the entire product line.

Business Expansion and Growth Performance

Marketing plays a vital role in expanding a company. Companies that are searching for avenues for expansion can use internal or external resources to reach their growth and business expansion goals.

Growth comes as the result of marketing efforts and the performance measurement of those efforts. Growth needs to be managed, cultivated, and tracked like a product. Growth doesn't just happen; it takes planning to produce controlled, diverse and consistent results.

Internal Growth

Although simple in theory, internal growth is generated through mixing and matching types of products, markets (geographic area), and customers. It allows you to create growth by building marketing strategies and tactics around the core elements of your business. Those elements are:

- new products or changes to current products

- new customers, former customers or current customers

- new business opportunities

Exhibit 3-1 displays the options you can mix together to increase growth through market/customer/product combinations.

Exhibit 3-1

Growth/Expansion Options

		Markets/Customers	
	New Products	New Markets	New Customer Types
			Current Customer Types
Products			Former Customer Types
	Current Products	Currrent Markets	New Customer Types
			Current Customer Types
			Former Customer Types

This exhibit illustrates growth through internal means. Internal implies using existing resources to obtain your growth goals. For example, if you obtained your goals in the past, why were you able to do so? You need to understand why growth did or did not happen internally so you can make changes to control it better in the future. Internal growth can be obtained by:

- selling more product—increased effort

- selling more product—more products available to sell

- lowering costs to produce products and/or the cost of marketing those products

- raising prices on products sold

External Growth

External growth comes as the result of business practices. As with internal growth, the purpose is to mix and match elements to produce growth. The elements can be entirely external or a combination of internal and external elements.

External growth relies on business relationships to produce sales. These relationships can provide added resources, and these resources, in turn, can produce growth through the efforts of others. Consider the following business resources and determine if they have be used and, if so, how effective these relationships have been.

- acquisition (new products from competitors)

- mergers

- franchising

- licensing (selling rights—all or limited)

- business relationship alignment (e.g., joint venture)

The objective of this section is to determine how you have been achieving growth (assuming you are). Then you can determine how to maintain and increase it in the future.

Marketing Organizational Performance

The infrastructure that supports the marketing management of your company consists of people, technology, and information. Experience, talent, education, leadership, and resources are all important in today's marketing environment, but these three infrastructure components are the main drivers. Marketing in the twenty-first century will depend on marketing and other departments working together as a team. It will require an investment in technology, such as powerful personal computers, on-line electronic data transfer, and Internet or intranet accessibility. Information will need to be at one's fingertips. It can be housed in a centralized data warehouse, but it must be available at the point of sale.

Modern marketing efforts must recognize and use these structure-building elements. The greatest strategies, tactics, and actions will fail if qualified staff are not on board, if information is not reported on a timely and insightful basis, or if the most up-to-date tools are not made available.

Organizational Structure—Proper Staffing

Try to understand your marketing "machine." Your marketing organization and operations establish the way you run your marketing activities. You need to address your personnel resources in terms of their ability to perform marketing duties. Begin by determining the level of activity being handled by your current marketing staff. Is your staff qualified? Do they need more training? If they are not able to perform the marketing work, should they be reassigned or terminated?

Capacity modeling will help you gauge your ability to handle the amount of business your company desires. To do this, you need to define the tasks needed to complete a process and then determine how long it takes to complete each task, the percentage of time a staffer needs to complete a task, and the number of staffers needed. Now you can assess how effective you are at managing your business and decide if changes such as outsourcing are needed.

After analyzing your staffing situation, ask yourself how you will adjust. Will you expand, downsize, or change job responsibilities? What will be the results? How will you evaluate the decisions? The following concerns may apply to your situation:

Expansions to Existing Staff

- new hires

- part-time/per project (e.g., outside marketing consultants)

- downsizing of existing staff

- restructuring

- shared job responsibilities

- reassignments

Changes in Existing Staff's Position Responsibilities

- promotions

- new position creations

- job responsibilities (duties and reporting changes)

- effect on costs (direct, not marketing expenses)

- compensation packages

- training

- other (e.g., incentives)

Organizational Structure—Proper Working Environment

Staffing is key, but providing the environment for staff to interact and produce results is equally important. Organizational structure is an environment that has been designed using structural and cultural attributes. The manner in which individuals are placed in the different areas of the marketing department, and other departments in the company, will promote or deflate marketing efforts.

The marketing department has evolved over the years, and as companies have progressed, so has the focus of the marketing department. Marketing has moved from a simple sales department to multifunction departments that balance all nine marketing functions. (Refer to the Marketing Mix Performance section later in this unit.) Today, an organization can be designed utilizing any of the following structural configurations:

- functionally oriented

- product-oriented

- market-oriented (geographic)

- hybrid (functional, product, and geographic combined)

- matrix or cross-functional

- process-based/team-oriented

The functional, product, market, and hybrid forms all use a top-to-bottom hierarchical flow that provides centralized control over marketing implementation. Exhibit 3-2 below displays examples of these forms.

The matrix, or cross-functional, forms and the process-based/team-oriented forms promote more freedom and innovation and empower staff to take ownership in their marketing efforts. Needless to say, these tend to be the organizational structures of choice, assuming management endorses not only the marketing department's approach, but also the involvement of the entire company. Exhibit 3-3 displays examples of these forms.

Exhibit 3-2

Functional/Product/Market/Hybrid Forms

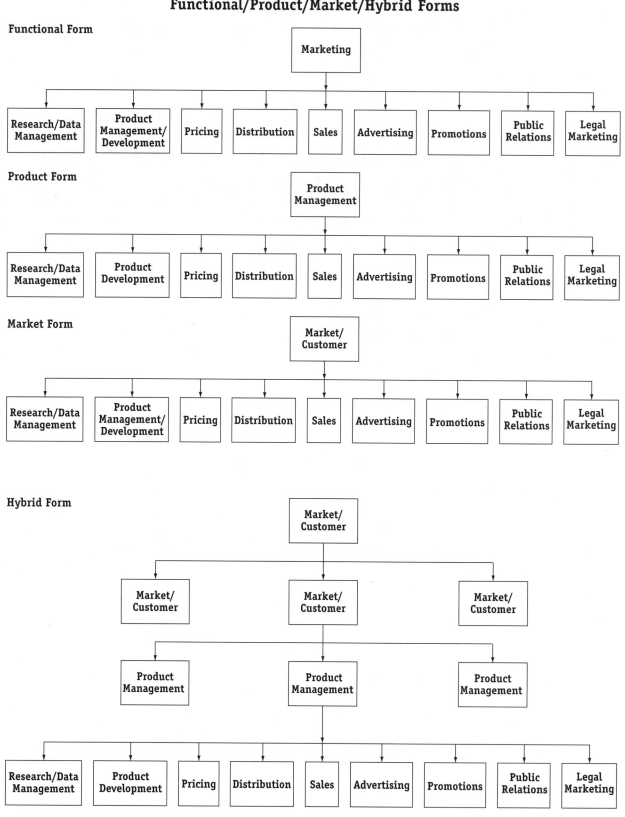

Functional Form

Marketing

- Research/Data Management
- Product Management/Development
- Pricing
- Distribution
- Sales
- Advertising
- Promotions
- Public Relations
- Legal Marketing

Product Form

Product Management

- Research/Data Management
- Product Development
- Pricing
- Distribution
- Sales
- Advertising
- Promotions
- Public Relations
- Legal Marketing

Market Form

Market/Customer

- Research/Data Management
- Product Management/Development
- Pricing
- Distribution
- Sales
- Advertising
- Promotions
- Public Relations
- Legal Marketing

Hybrid Form

Market/Customer

- Market/Customer
- Market/Customer
- Market/Customer

Product Management (three)

- Research/Data Management
- Product Development
- Pricing
- Distribution
- Sales
- Advertising
- Promotions
- Public Relations
- Legal Marketing

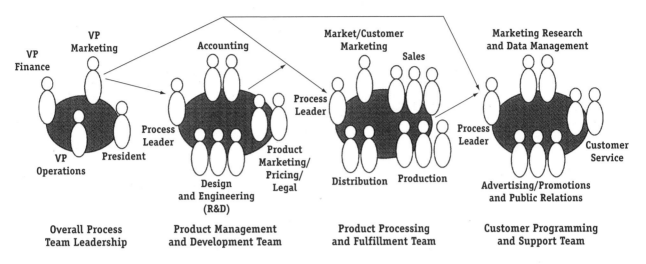

Exhibit 3-3

Modern Forms—Process-Based Structures

Overall Process Team Leadership — **Product Management and Development Team** — **Product Processing and Fulfillment Team** — **Customer Programming and Support Team**

Although the more traditional forms are still effective, especially in small companies, the more modern forms are taking the lead in marketing departments today. A department typically builds a customer/product-oriented process by reformulating old hierarchical forms that are still functional in their design. Once everyone has adjusted to the matrix/cross-functional world, the company and the marketing department totally redesign their roles and responsibilities into a process-based/team-oriented environment. In this situation, the processes become the stars of the company, not the functional departments. Each process is based on a customer/product business flow, and teams are arranged according to key stages of operations. This configuration promotes direct interaction on a process, instead of linking back to a function or department authority.

Process-driven organizations tend to respond faster to market needs because they are decentralized and closer to the action. Process-, team-, or matrix/cross-functional-oriented structures not only promote productivity, but also improve information systems, finance/accounting (reporting), and quality control.

Organizational Structure—Roles and Responsibilities

Once you've established your current and new organizational structure, you need to define the positions assigned to the structure. The focus is not to determine who reports to whom, but who does what with whom. The key is to isolate on the individual activities and tasks the marketing staff will carry out in the marketing tactics and actions. The following example offers ideas for dealing with relationship issues in organizational structure.

Standard staff-level position in marketing

- duties (activities and parameters)
- relationship with other marketing staffers

- relationship with their assigned marketing manager and other marketing managers
- relationship with other department (non-marketing) managers and their staffers

Standard management-level position in marketing

- duties (activities and parameters)
- relationship with other marketing managers
- relationship with assigned manager
- relationship with marketing staff
- relationship with nonmarketing managers and their staff

The personnel aspect of organizational management also takes into account core competencies that the staff must either possess or be willing to obtain. Job qualifications would focus on market- or industry-specific capabilities as well as marketing and management capabilities. Market- or industry-specific capabilities would center on industry knowledge. Marketing and management capabilities would comprise marketing skills and professional conduct.

Position assignments will follow the actions determined by the structure you select. The number of positions will depend on the size of the company, stage of its life cycle, resources, and the type of industry it is in. In any case, your audit should focus on the activities and tasks assigned to individuals and if they have the capabilities to carry out their charge.

Cultural Elements in Organizational Structure

It is not enough to address how your organization is or should be structured; you must consider the culture as well. *Culture* is an environment that is fostered to enable individuals to cooperate in producing quality work. It is the behavior of an organization. The culturally correct marketing structure of the new millennium focuses on staff becoming entrepreneurial, teamwork-oriented, proactive, empowered, and customer-driven. These attributes create a healthy marketing environment that is flexible, acceptable to change, and cost effective.

Processes and Procedures

The management of an organization's structure and culture centers around rules. That doesn't mean organizations must be rigid and controlling. It does mean that guidelines and, when needed, rules must be in place and followed in operating any effective marketing group.

Process and procedures include:

- processes (flow of business through the organizational structure)

- procedures (written step-by-step documentation of the processes)

- policies (decision ruling on procedures—when needed)

- controls and corrective actions (tracking/reporting to meet predetermined levels of acceptance standards with penalties for not meeting standards and reacceptance actions to meet those standards)

Exhibit 3-4 uses a process flow to illustrate the relationship of processes and procedures. It displays how a department manages its functions (three examples provided) and what activities (four examples provided) it assigns to each function. The example shows how a department/function/activity receives, performs, and completes a marketing task or action. The process is that step-by-step effort

Exhibit 3-4

Process Flow

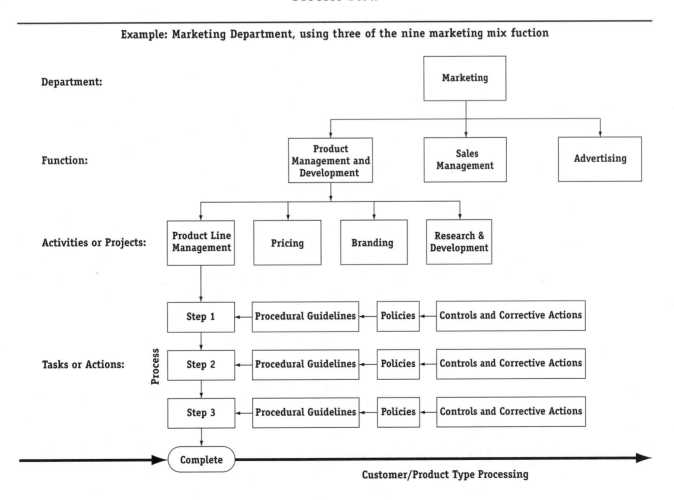

Example: Marketing Department, using three of the nine marketing mix fuction

needed to complete that task or action, with the corresponding procedures, policies (where needed), controls, and corrective actions. This example is based on a horizontal hybrid organizational structure in which different products drive the processing of each product as it relates to the customer.

The final analysis of your audit is to assess how effective your marketing organization has been. If changes are needed, the options provided will give ideas for reshaping your marketing department.

Technology and Information Management

After reviewing your marketing organization, you are ready to address your ability to handle information. This includes accessibility of information to your marketing staff and customers. To accomplish this analysis, you need to audit your ability to generate timely, detailed, and accurate data on your marketing efforts. This includes reviewing your ability to house and distribute data that identify customers and their needs. Whether you call it a sales automation system, lead management system, marketing information system (MIS), selling delivery system, or data warehouse/database marketing system, you must have the technology and the logic processes to produce usable marketing information.

The first thing to focus on is the centralized information source or database. This includes reviewing what information is being collected, how it is collected and organized (manually or on-line), and how it is used. The next order of business is to determine if the technology being used (software, hardware, communication linkages, expert staff, etc.) is adequate to support your marketing needs. Once you have assessed your marketing information needs and resources, you can determine how effectively you are managing your marketing information.

Marketing Data Usage

Your initial review establishes your ability to collect and manage marketing data. Now you need to determine the many uses for your data. As always, your data will be used to monitor and influence forces impacting you from market, customer, product, and marketing management points of view. These forces include the processes that support the sales cycle: defining, identifying, contacting, capturing, and servicing the customer.

Following are potential uses for your marketing information:

- sales reporting

- performance measurement (e.g., productivity, business generation, costing, etc.)

- order processing

- pricing and product information

- competitor intelligence

- lead generation, distribution, and performance tracking

- production, inventory, and shipping reporting

- customer inquiries, satisfaction, and complaint response measurement

- marketing cost accounting

- prospect/customer activity (pipeline) tracking

- database management and marketing (storage, retrieval, and sales transactions)

- database management and marketing (data collection)

- marketing mix performance tracking

Each of these may or may not apply to your situation. Each suggested use can stand alone or be part of one interrelated information system. These uses can be fleshed out into subareas that pertain to your specific business, customer, or marketing environment.

In today's marketing arena, managing customers is essential. This means your systems and processes are built around the customer and your products are oriented toward customer needs. If you can prepare your business to reach those customers, you will be ahead of the game. This is a very important point in this book—everything in marketing today is driven by electronic data control and transfer. An effective marketer knows how to harness and manage the power of marketing information for the purposes of entering, arranging, verifying, and selecting data. The ability to direct customers to your products, stimulate a purchase, and estimate buying or problem patterns is critical to the success of your strategies, tactics, and actions.

Evaluate your marketing technology and information management capabilities to determine if upgrades are needed. If so, you need to design, build, and manage systems and processes that will augment your marketing endeavors. Exhibit 3-5 shows how two companies manage their marketing information.

Analyzing Internal Communications

Communication within your company is a vital part of its day-to-day operations, although misunderstandings invariably occur. This section addresses awareness of information, not good listening techniques. In analyzing your present internal communications practices, the main things to consider are control and consistency. Whatever you transmit, you need to maintain standard formats; this will easily alert you to a mistake or a miscommunication. Consider communications patterns over the last three and the next three years within your marketing department, with other departments, with other business units, and with corporate headquarters.

Exhibit 3-5

Marketing System, Example 1

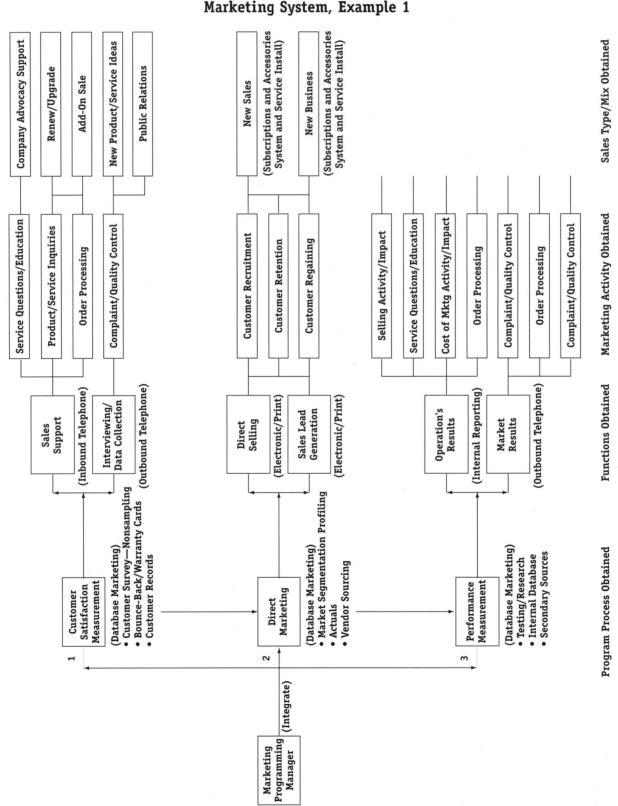

Exhibit 3-5

Marketing System, Example 2

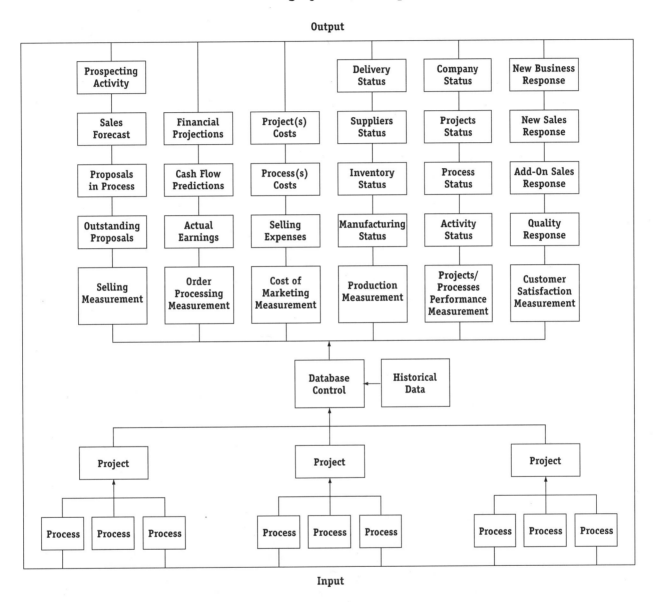

The secret to good marketing communications is to keep it simple and direct, but with substance and relevance.

Marketing Strategy—Thinking and Planning Performance

The next area of inquiry looks at how your marketing department forms its marketing strategies and programs its overall tactical directions. The findings you compile from the audit will enable you to identify needs, problems, and opportunities in your marketing efforts. Then you can convert that information into a strategic marketing plan and an annual tactical marketing plan.

Strategic Marketing Management

What are your core initiatives? What are your key strategies? Do they match the strategies of the company? These are some of the questions you need to ask yourself to determine the strategic course of the business/marketing department. Your audit needs to outline the process you go through to establish your strategies and assess the relevance and impact of those strategies.

To arrive at a strategy, you must first develop a mission, goals, and measurable objectives.

The book *Developing Successful Marketing Strategies* in this Toolbox series provides definitions for each step in this process.

Your strategies must: represent the vision of your organization to improve or exceed at some marketing attribute or capability; touch all areas where you are strong or weak; demonstrate ideas, yet be solid and accountable; be visionary, but obtainable in one or two years. They must be measurable, seek improvement, and obtain a competitive edge or growth through products, customers, markets, and marketing management elements.

Tactical Marketing Management

Although the next sections focus on the core elements of an annual tactical marketing plan (in terms of actions), the key here is the relationship with strategic thought. The tactical plan is the real meat of marketing. Strategy defines what is to be accomplished. Tactics deliver the strategy by carrying out the actions needed to make thought a reality.

Your goal in this section of your audit is to see if your marketing strategies relate to the company's overall strategies. If so, do your annual marketing tactics reflect your strategies? Do your tactics meet your mission, goals, and objectives? If not, your analysis is unclear. If you are doing these things, there may be room for improvement. The key issue in this section is to make sure you are organizing your marketing thoughts in a way that moves your business forward.

Marketing Mix Performance

The heart of the Unit 3 audit is the marketing mix. This section deals with the mechanisms that market your products. These tactics tell you how, when, where, and to whom you are directing your marketing efforts and resources. They should reflect your overall marketing strategies and link to your forecasts.

All of the marketing functions should work together to fit in the overall marketing plan, but they should be programmed as individual plans to complement the other functional plans. As a marketer, your job is to determine which activities you are using and how effectively your mix has performed. As you go through the functions (overall and individually), ask yourself the following questions:

- Are the marketing mix functions integrated?

- Do they use technology and automated systems?

- Do they use innovative methods to reach, capture, and keep customers?

- Do they pursue current customers as vigorously as new and former customers?

- Do they use customer life cycle or relationship marketing?

- Do they focus on bringing products to customers versus bringing customers to products?

- Do they make money? Is there growth and improvement from year to year?

- Do they save money or maintain costs while producing more?

- Do they use point-of-sale marketing methods?

If you see a lot of nos, consider making changes!

Review the nine marketing functions discussed next to determine where changes (if any) are needed. Keep in mind the questions above.

Marketing Mix Performance—Marketing Research and Data Management

As mentioned in the Technology and Information Management section, the management of marketing effectiveness, customer needs, product performance, and market change depends on solid information. The act of research and the management of the data collected through the use of technology is what this section is all about.

In the past, marketing research focused on information gleaned from the traditional instruments of data collection, tabulation, and analysis. That is still true, but those procedures have been augmented by the use of technology and electronic data. Today, marketing researchers are much more than statistical experts; they are PC-based database managers. They build data banks of the various marketing drivers, variables, or data points that provide insight into one's marketing approach. As you examine your marketing research efforts, keep in mind not only the methods, but the use of automated or electronic data systems from which much of marketing data originate.

Research Plan Evaluation

To this point, we have been discussing how to research the markets you are in or intend to be in and the products you are offering or will offer. Now research takes on a different role; here it is used to understand the marketing mix functions and to direct marketing mix efforts at meeting business goals. Marketing research in this situation is an ongoing business process that monitors the factors that could influence your marketing plan. It is here that customer satisfaction, advertising research, economic impact, sales effectiveness, and product testing take place.

The marketing research process is probably the only marketing function that is more an art than a science or process; for that reason we provide examples of how you might approach collecting, tabulating, analyzing, and applying marketing-related research. You will have to take the concepts shared in this section and apply them to your specific situation.

In understanding your research activities at this level, you need to identify what types of research you did in the past and what you are presently doing. You also need to understand results generated from that research and whether they affected your marketing actions favorably. You need to determine budget (Format 87), types of research performed (Format 88), types of research techniques used (Format 89), types of research methods used (Format 90), types of research instruments used (Format 91), and how the analysis and reporting procedures were handled (Format 92). These formats provide processes for evaluating how you have conducted your marketing activities. Complete each format for the last three and the next three years by using the outlines provided.

Marketing Research Budget

Format 87 provides a method of establishing what you have spent on marketing research, by product. Complete the format by placing the costs for each product in the columns and then totaling those amounts.

Format 87

Marketing Research Budget

Activity	20___ Costs ($)	Percentage of Sales	20___ Costs ($)	Percentage of Sales	20___ Costs ($)	Percentage of Sales
ABC	10,000	5.0	11,000	6.0	5,000	4.0
ABC2	5,000	3.0	7,000	4.0	10,000	6.0
Total	15,000	8.0	18,000	10.0	15,000	10.0

Types of Research Used

The objective of this exercise is to establish what research projects you have undertaken. You need to identify research activities to assess their effects on individual products, the product line, and customer types. Using Format 88, consider the following types of research over the last three and the next three years:

- customer satisfaction

- product testing

- customer/market testing

- marketing mix/function testing (e.g., advertising tracking)

- other (i.e., lead list effectiveness)

Format 88		
Types of Research Performed (Tactics)		
20___		
By Product	**Types of Research Performed**	**Results**
ABC	Customer satisfaction to measure how well the product has performed	Approved customer perception
ABC2	Sales promotion research to track the success of couponing	Still collecting data
By Overall Product Line	Research has been conducted at a steady pace.	Improvements have been made as a result of research conducted.

Types of Research Techniques Used

The objective of this exercise is to establish what techniques you have used in conducting your research. You need to identify these activities to assess the effects on individual products, your product line, and customer types. Using Format 89, consider the following research techniques over the last three and next three years:

- primary

- secondary

- internal database

- auditing

Format 89

Types of Research Techniques Used

20___

By Product	Types of Research Techniques Used	Results
ABC	Primary	Will continue to use
ABC2	Primary and secondary	Same
By Overall Product Line	Primary and secondary	Same, but will investigate database

---

Types of Research Methods Used

The objective of this exercise is to establish what methods you have used to conduct your research. You need to identify these activities to assess their effects on your individual products, the product line, and customer types. Using Format 90, consider the following methods used over the last three and the next three years:

- qualitative

- quantitative

- statistical

- nonstatistical (e.g., expert opinion)

Format 90

Types of Research Methods Used

20___

By Product	Types of Research Methods Used	Results
ABC	Quantitative only	Data limited
ABC2	Qualitative and quantitative	Good balance
By Overall Product Line	Both	Tried many different methods

Types of Research Instruments Used

The objective of this exercise is to establish what types of research instruments you have used. You need to identify these activities to assess their effects on individual products, your product line, and customer types. Using Format 91, consider the following research instruments used over the last three and the next three years:

- intercept (e.g., mall interviews)/one-on-one

- focus groups

- survey (mail or telephone)

- other

Format 91		
Types of Research Instruments Used		
20___		
By Product	**Types of Research Instruments Used**	**Results**
ABC	Mall one-on-one interviews	Gave good insight to key issues
ABC2	Same and focus groups	Same
By Overall Product Line	Used a mixture	Same

Types of Tabulation and Analysis Used

The objective of this exercise is to establish what types of tabulation and analysis activities you used to understand your research data. You need to identify these activities to assess their effects on individual products, your product line, and customer types. Using Format 92, consider the following forms of tabulation and analysis used over the past three and the next three years:

- cross-tabulation/summary tabulation (standard)

- statistical modeling analysis

- other

Format 92		
Types of Tabulation and Analysis Used		
20___		
By Product	**Types of Tabulation and Analysis Used**	**Results**
ABC	Standard	Limited, but useful
ABC2	Standard	Limited, but useful
By Overall Product Line	Standard	Limited, but useful

Resulting Changes Made to Marketing Plans

The objective of this exercise is to establish how your marketing actions changed (if at all) as a result of research. The key is to show how the data affected your marketing plans. Using Format 93, consider the following types of changes to your marketing plans:

- impact analysis

- adjustment of marketing tactics (including all related strategies)

- impact on marketing research

Format 93		
Changes Made to Marketing Plans		
20___		
By Product	**Effect on Marketing Plans**	**Results**
ABC	Changed formula slightly to make it smell better.	Changed advertising and sales increased.
ABC2	Waiting	Waiting
By Overall Product Line	Changes were small, but important.	Customers responded favorably to changes.

Marketing Data Management

The technology aspect of marketing was audited in a previous section. Now you are auditing how that technology is applied in managing your marketing data. You need to review how you are entering and updating data, storing and retrieving data, using data, and measuring the effectiveness of the data. Ask yourself the following questions:

- Does the architecture of the database (software) handle the marketing tasks you routinely must support?

- Does the storage capacity handle the amount of data you are required to manipulate? Does it perform this activity quickly?

- Does the statistical application provide you with the insights to make solid marketing decisions?

- Does your database play a major role in targeting customers, uncovering customer needs, predicting customer demand, and determining when purchases will most likely occur?

- What type of data do you house? What is the source (identification, accuracy, and timeliness) of the data?

- How is the data reported? Who has access to input and read-only key marketing information?

It is a good idea to secure a systems expert or consultant to aid you in managing your marketing data.

Marketing Mix Performance—Product Management

In Unit 2, your audit focused on the product element of marketing management. In that role, the audit focused on assessing a value or a level of contribution to profitability and volume of business. In the marketing mix role, you are evaluating how effective you have been in marketing these products. Your objective here is to review how various changes in a product or product line, or changes to other marketing mix functions (e.g., advertising) in support of your products, have hurt or helped the performance of your products. The terms *product* and *service* are the same when speaking of a product as the core purpose of a business's existence. A service, however, can be a support resource used as an additional income source or as a support benefit. In this section we are focusing attention on the core product type from which the audit will be conducted.

Budgeting Considerations

The first area of concern is your marketing budget for product management. The costs you will incur here are normally associated with product development expenses. Depending how your company allocates product development costs (marketing and other departments), your cost structure may differ. The goal is to establish some standard from which past and present product expenses can be measured. (See Format 94.)

Format 94

Product Management Budget

Activity	20___ Costs ($)	Percentage of Sales	20___ Costs ($)	Percentage of Sales	20___ Costs ($)	Percentage of Sales
ABC Product update	20,000	2.0	—	0	—	0
ABC2 Product introduction	30,000	3.0	30,000	3.0	—	0
Total	50,000	5.0	30,000	3.0	—	0

Changes to Product/Product Line

The goal with this segment is to profile the changes attempted, why they were attempted, and the results that were realized. In describing your existing product line management, consider the following issues over the last three and the next three years:

- cost reductions
- product alterations—upgrades, enhancements, refinements, etc.
- repositioning (market or product line)
- changes to marketing approach (e.g., private labeling)
- eliminations
- price increases/decreases
- volume increases/decreases
- service enhancements (income or support)

Use Format 95 to record the tactics that have had an impact on your individual products and the entire product line.

Format 95

Existing Product Line Tactics

By Product	Existing Product Line Strategies	Results
ABC	Altered product formula to make it smell better.	Sales increased by 5% within 6 months, remained steady.
ABC2	No change	No change
By Overall Product Line	Modified products to reflect changes in consumer needs.	Enhanced product performance.

Changes to Other Marketing Mix Functions

As you did with your existing products, you need to isolate new product ideas and introductions to determine your level of success. Consider product introductions developed in-house or acquired over the last three and the next three years. These would include:

- replacements
- additions
- alternative income sources

- service enhancements (income or support)

- product acquisition (another company's products)

Use Format 96 to record your new product line strategies.

Format 96		
New Product Line Tactics		
By Product	**New Product Line Strategies**	**Results**
ABC	Does not apply	Does not apply
ABC2	Developed through own R&D activities through analysis of ABC product's strengths & weaknesses.	No change
By Overall Product Line	Kept all new product efforts in house while considering competitors acquisitions.	Product changes were small.

Branding Changes (for Consumer Package Product or Service Industries Only)

In many cases, product and brand are the same, but in the event you separate the two, branding changes need to be reviewed and evaluated. Branding changes are measures taken to develop a product's identity, name, or image. Additional issues to be considered over the last three and the next three years include:

- brand developing

- brand reinforcing

- brand repositioning

- brand modifications

Branding activities are vital to a product's existence in the consumer package product and service industries because a product's identification and branding transmit a message to the customer: "Buy me!" Use Format 97 to record branding tactics that have affected your product line changes:

Packaging Changes (for Consumer Package Product or Service Industries Only)

As an extension of branding, packaging plays a crucial role in imaging, name recognition, and identity. In the consumer market, packaging is the physical extension of your branding. The package that surrounds, protects, or contains

Format 97		
Branding Tactics		
By Product	**Branding Strategies**	**Results**
ABC	Repositioned brand identity to reflect new formula that addresses "pine" smell trend.	Attracted new customers, sales improved 10% in one year.
ABC2	No changes	No changes
By Overall Product Line	Modified branding to meet the needs of customers seeking specific features.	Products are better, perceived as positive.

your product must convey your brand identity. Use Format 98 to record packaging tactics, taking the following issues into account:

- communications approach (i.e., message)
- usefulness of package
- cost of packaging, shipping, and delivery
- appearance of package at point of sale

Format 98		
Packaging Tactics		
By Product	**Packaging Strategies**	**Results**
ABC	Changes made on package to announce formula changes and explain the improvement.	Customers appreciated change.
ABC2	None	None
By Overall Product Line	Enhance current packaging to demonstrate product responsiveness to customer demands.	Overall, products benefited in terms of value.

Service Enhancements

Service before, during, and after the sale of a product is very important. The service a customer receives is a value-added characteristic for your product. Use Format 99 to record service enhancements you have adopted to boost customer assistance for your product or product line.

Marketing Mix Performance—Pricing

Although price is integrated into your product management, and usually there is very little cost associated with pricing, pricing should be analyzed separately

Format 99		
Service Enhancements		
By Product	Service Enhancements	Results
ABC	New support line to help customers effectively use the product.	Callers expressed a few problems but enjoyed having a source for questions.
ABC2	None	None
By Overall Product Line	Continue to offer value-added capabilities for product customers	Customers are more loyal to products due to support help.

because of its importance to every single marketing move. The pricing element establishes what it will take for a buyer to obtain your product.

In Unit 2, pricing was audited in relation to profit and the value of your products. In this section you will assess how effective your pricing is at marketing your products. Your audit addresses how the pricing function works with other marketing mix functions to sell products. It looks at how your past and present pricing policies were set and how effective they are. It also evaluates your current pricing tactics.

The first element to address in evaluating your pricing is your budget. Format 100 considers price as a function of your budget. Depending upon how you allocate your marketing dollars, you most likely will have no pricing budget per se. Your pricing efforts will usually fall under the research or product management budget. In any event, a pricing budget format has been provided if you desire to use it.

Format 100					
Pricing Budget					
Product	20___ Costs ($)	Percentage of Sales	20___ Costs ($)	Percentage of Sales	20___ Costs ($)	Percentage of Sales
ABC	None	0	None	0	None	0
ABC2	None	0	None	0	None	0
Total	—	0	—	0	—	0

Pricing Formula Criteria

The criteria to be considered in Format 101 will help you establish your pricing formula. These criteria, to be traced over the last three and the next three years, include:

- cost (total: gross vs. net)

- market demand (price × frequency × volume × set time period = demand)

Cost can be defined on many levels and include many things. As a general rule, you can figure both gross and net prices based on cost, but you work primarily with net prices. Costs will help you determine the base price you need to charge. Market demand is more difficult to measure. While cost sets your floor (base), market demand sets your ceiling (maximum). You need to establish what the market will accept by looking at product research data, competitors' pricing programs, and the product life cycle. Use Format 101 to record your pricing criteria.

Format 101

Pricing Formula Criteria

By Product (per unit)	Base	Range	Maximum	20___
ABC	$12.95	($7.05)	$20.00	
ABC2	$13.99	($5.96)	$19.95	
By Overall Product Line	$13.47	($6.51)	$19.98	

Setting Product Line Pricing Policies

This section is the core tactical area which outlines the pricing policies you have established. Pricing policies include the tactical actions you have taken and the procedures you have employed to protect the integrity of your price points. In this section, you are concentrating on discounting, incentives, and planned allowances. These three areas will influence your customer to purchase and can help to prevent unforeseen losses from impacting the profitability of your products.

In Format 102, you will consider the following tactics over the last three and the next three years:

- base price

- discounting (volume points)

- allowances (for losses)

- special pricing (limited time offers)

- price positioning (lower, higher, and same as the competition)

- price promotions (to move product quickly)

Format 102	
Price Tactics	
20___	
By Product	**Pricing Activities**
ABC	*No discounts with the exception of lower prices used to sell inventory when the product is replaced.*
ABC2	*Price set just slightly higher than ABC to reflect its higher grade.*
By Overall Product Line	*Pricing very stable, not open to price wars and/or price changes.*

Price/Cost Structure

In Unit 2, the price/cost structure was audited to establish the level of profitability for individual products and your total product line. In this section, you are concerned with specific elements of that price/cost structure. Those elements are discounting and allowances. The section above addressed these two elements as tactics. Here you are isolating on the process by which you arrived at the dollar figures that drive discounting and allowance tactics.

To arrive at your numbers, you will probably use customized models in which you play what-if games with these pricing elements. However, you most likely will look at your pricing elements in relation to:

- volume (dollars and units)

- losses (dollars and units) and the reasons why losses occurred

- quantities of products for discounting (dollars and units)

Format 103 provides a place to establish your price/cost structure for each product and overall product·line over the last three and the next three years. Remember, you don't have to build in these pricing adjustments if they are not needed. If you do wish to use them, you can use one or both.

Marketing Mix Performance—Distribution

The function of distribution used to be easy to define. Today, with the various interactive systems and multiple channel options, distribution is no longer a quick plan. On-line inventory tracking, automated fulfillment, and transportation advancements are changing the face of distribution. Distribution options differ in the consumer package product, business-to-business/industrial manufacturing, and service industries.

The role of distribution also varies in the different industries. In the consumer package product industry, distribution's role is complex because of the

Format 103

Price/Cost Structure—Discounts and Allowances

20___

	Product: ABC			Product: ABC2		
Volume (Units)	1 to 5	6 to 10	11 +	1 to 5	6 to 10	11 +
Price ($)	$100.00	$100.00	$100.00	$150.00	$150.00	$150.00
Discount ($)	$0	$10.00	$20.00	$0	$10.00	$20.00
Allowance ($)	$1.00	$2.00	$3.00	$2.00	$4.00	$6.00
Subtotal	$1.00	$12.00	$23.00	$2.00	$14.00	$26.00
Revenue ($)	$99.00	$88.00	$77.00	$148.00	$136.00	$124.00

changes in retailing. No longer do specialty stores or local store chains rule the landscape. Today, category killers like Lowes or Office Depot direct the business approach in the modern world of marketing.

Essentially, a distribution plan in the consumer package product industry will consist of the following delivery system options:

- producer directly to the customer
- producer to a retailer and then to the customer
- producer to a wholesaler, then to a retailer, and then to the customer
- producer to an agent (e.g., manufacturer's rep), then to a wholesaler, then to a retailer, and finally to the customer

In the business-to-business/industrial manufacturing industry, your role as a business can be either a producer or the distribution source itself. Your primary options are as follows:

- producer to the industrial user
- producer to a distributor or dealer and then to the industrial user
- producer to an agent and then to the industrial user

Historically, the service industries omitted distribution issues in their marketing plans because a service is intangible and distribution was nonexistent. However, distribution can be interpreted as any manner in which a service is delivered to a customer. For example, the transmission of data (electronic data transfer) or signals to produce an action can be considered a type of distribution. As a result, distribution can be included as part of a service-based marketing plan.

Budgets

Depending on how your company defines distribution, your budget may include warehousing, shipping, and transportation or just one or two of those areas. The life stages of your products will assist you in defining your specific distribution plans. (See Format 104.)

Format 104

Distribution Budget

Product	20___ Costs ($)	Percentage of Sales	20___ Costs ($)	Percentage of Sales	20___ Costs ($)	Percentage of Sales
ABC	15,000	1.5	15,000	1.5	16,000	1.6
ABC2	16,000	1.6	16,500	1.7	17,000	1.7
Total	31,000	3.1	31,500	3.2	33,000	3.3

Once your budget is established, your next step is to determine how well defined your prior distribution objectives have been. This assessment should include such items as coverage, outlet types, timing, and direct or indirect delivery.

Selecting Delivery Channels

To this point you have been determining what you are offering to customers. Now you must identify how to get your offerings into their hands in the most cost-effective and efficient way. In selecting the channel options, you are essentially selecting the tactical element of your distribution plan. Therefore, the following three steps and the options available therein, represent the tactical side of your distribution plan.

First, *review your delivery system* in light of the options outlined earlier. In selecting a delivery system, consider the relationship with sales and other departments (e.g., inventory). If a sales automation system is being employed, distribution will play a major role in that system. Delivery systems for inventory fulfillment and shipping can be semiautomated or fully automated electronic on-line delivery systems.

Second, *verify the method of delivery*. This aspect of your distribution plan addresses the physical manner in which the product or service is delivered. The following options are available for transportation or transmission:

- highway, railroad, water or air carrier

- under-/over ground flow

- electronic transfer

Finally, *identify the destination* where you have been shipping your product for purchase. Indirect destinations include:

- distributors

- dealers and resellers

- other manufacturers

- franchise

- brokers/agents

- telemarketing and fulfillment operator

Direct destination methods include:

- person-to-person (door-to-door)

- mail order (catalogs, TV home shopping)

- automatic vending

- internet, on-line services, and interactive/point-of-purchase kiosks

- retail outlets (department store, specialty store, etc.)

- wholesale outlets (category killers, factory outlets, wholesale showrooms, etc.)

Another option is a joint venture in which companies share the distribution and marketing efforts. This is often used in private label arrangements where identical products are marketed under different names.

Use Formats 105 and 106 to analyze delivery channels and distribution tactics.

Format 105
Channel Selections

20___	
By Product	**Channel Selections**
ABC	Shipped to retail specialty and department stores via distribution centers.
ABC2	Shipped directly to retail stores and sold through select catalog vendors who receive product as ordered.
By Overall Product Line	Products distributed through standard channels as well as special avenues, as needed.

Format 106	
Distribution Tactics	
20___	
By Product	**Distribution Strategies**
ABC	*Shipped to distributors who then ship to retail outlets. Price incentives given if sold by a certain time.*
ABC2	*Shipped to distributor and vendor to be delivered to outlets and direct to consumers.*
By Overall Product Line	*Distribution performed by selecting the channels that deliver products in a timely fashion at low cost.*

Remember the following key points:

- Select distribution options.

- Mix and match those options into distribution tactics.

- Balance tactics with sales, production, inventory control and operations.

Contracts Awarded and Status

Finally, identify your distribution methods by name and method of delivery. Who is transporting and delivering your products? How and when are their contracts awarded? You need to track your relationships with outside firms, including the status of contracts with suppliers, shippers, warehousing facilities, and, delivery or installation services.

Marketing Mix Performance—Sales Management and Selling

Selling is the action that holds your marketing plan together. Although selling plays a key role in the success of your marketing plans, marketing activities should not be aimed solely toward sales and salespeople. Sales should be balanced with the other eight marketing functions to form a well-supported and integrated marketing plan. Selling options differ in the consumer package product, business-to-business/industrial manufacturing, and service industries.

The Internet, on-line sales automation, and laptop PC technology are changing how sales are made, but the goals and principles are the same.

The sales management process starts with deciding who sells your products and how they do it; in other words, sales force development. Motivating your sales force by means of incentives and compensation for their performance based on quotas is next. Then you must establish how they have been selling, to what customers they have been selling, and how large their sales territory is in terms of physical area or key accounts. Finally, you need to establish how you have managed these salespeople, the sales they generated, and their overall sales performance.

Sales and Selling Budgeting

Review your budget to determine if it reflects your commitment to meeting your goals. Your budget should include everything except compensation (base or bonus)—that is covered in either your marketing operational budget or your company's overall overhead expenses. Format 107 will help you track what you spend on the management of your sales over the coming year.

Format 107

Sales Management Budget

Activity	20___ Costs ($)	Percentage of Sales	20___ Costs ($)	Percentage of Sales	20___ Costs ($)	Percentage of Sales
ABC	20,000	2.0	22,000	2.2	22,000	2.2
ABC2	21,000	2.1	23,000	2.3	24,000	2.4
Total*	41,000	4.1	45,000	4.5	46,000	4.6

*Total budget does *not* include salesperson's compensation.

Sales Systems Selection

In the past, sales systems were defined as the process of prospecting, presenting, closing, and delivering the desired goods. Today, sales systems are integrated, on-line computer systems that enable salespeople to market a product at the push of a button (almost). No longer do salespeople prospect; today they field inquiries and service customers.

A salesperson today can make a sales call armed with a complete record of the customer's sales history, up-to-date information about the customer's market and competitors, detailed product specifications, current (by the minute) price sheets and inventory reports, and all other data needed to close the sale. This is all possible with the availability of powerful portable computers that hold huge amounts of information, high-speed modems, cellular hookups, wireless transmission, and cutting-edge software. With a direct on-line link to the home office, a salesperson can place real-time orders.

Sales automation systems integrate research and data management, advertising (using direct marketing/response), distribution, and customer service to identify the customer and the customer's behavior. The end result is a system that balances modern technology with the human interaction of customer demand in a package that meets your sales goals.

Another form of sales system is the totally electronic "expert system." It relies on preprogrammed logic that auto-decisions a customer's likelihood of becoming a closed sale. It has artificial intelligence to define and select customers who will buy your products.

Using technology and information management resources, your sales automation system should be built with the help of a vendor, using fully integrated components that focus on the following key elements:

- database management (list selection/data acquisition and merging, customer identification, and purchasing predictions)

- sales/lead generation (inquiry production, distribution, and reporting)

- order processing (order entry, accounts receivable, shipping, inventory change reporting, and fulfillment/follow-up communications)

- customer support and services (satisfaction, call management, and problem reporting)

Exhibit 3-6 offers a plan (components needed) for a sales automation system, in terms of features.

Exhibit 3-6

Sales Automation System Example

Project Overview (elements for consideration)

I.   **Identify customer type to lead process**

    A.   Establish lead acquisition and management processes

        1.   Current customer to product matching

        2.   New customer to product matching

        3.   List/source selection and screening

    B.   Establish customer definition

        1.   Customer profiling—market segmentation situation (customer relationship management)

        2.   Customer profiling—credit quality/financial situation

    C.   Establish lead processing

        1.   Lead coding and tracking

        2.   Lead resolution tracking (active/inactive, close/sale, turndown, referral or unsolicited/solicited, inquiry response, new/current/former customer, etc.)

        3.   Lead performance tracking (cost per lead, response, sale/lead)

        4.   Lead distribution

continued

Exhibit 3-6 *(continued)*

Sales Automation System Example

II.   Identify lead-to-sales process (on-line access to information)

    A.   Establish product-selling system
1. Prospecting and interviewing
2. Close
3. Competitor, product specifications, pricing updates
4. Customer data (if current)

    B.   Establish production, sales, and service
1. Manufacturing
2. Marketing and sales
3. Distribution and customer service
4. Customer support

    C.   Establish reporting performances
1. Lead activity (amount and distribution)
2. Sales activity
3. Loan processing Production Activity
4. Marketing costing
5. Product and customer profitability
6. Compliance and corporate audit standards

III.   Identify sales to customer service process

    A.   Customer management
1. Customer inquiries and retention
2. Satisfaction research
3. Compliance management and problem solving

    B.   Servicing
1. Billing and payments
2. Payouts and closeouts
3. Collections

    C.   Technology usage and support
1. Internet access (on-line link or point-of-marketing tool)
2. Remote electronic channels (ATMs, ALMs, etc.)
3. System service (data and hardware)

Sales Management Structure

After assessing the system in which you have been operating your sales activities, you need to look at, the structure in which that system has been operating. The structure is the orientation of your sales efforts. It is important to define how you have been approaching sales and selling. Following are the options you may wish to check:

- product sales approach
- market sales approach

- customer-specific approach

- sales transaction approach

- combination approach

The trick is to determine which approach has been most successful. Which one responds the quickest to market, product, and customer issues? Which one has been the most productive and efficient in generating sales? Obviously, the customer approach, or an approach that features customer management, is a key marketing driver. The implications of your structure relate back to the system you have selected.

Marketing and Sales Management

Although we said that structure concentrates on how you arrange your sales department, it also refers to how your sales department is managed. There can be no more divisive or critical issue in marketing management than sales management.

The issue is should the marketing manager manage the sales manager, should they be equal, or should sales manage marketing? Although each structure has been successful, the one that provides the most consistent control, low risk, and balance is the one in which the marketing manager manages the sales manager. Marketers have argued about this relationship for years, but when sales managers control how the other marketing mix functions operate, you get a slanted view of marketing. If sales runs marketing, you typically get low-priced products that may not be profitable but are easy to sell. If marketing runs sales, you get a more balanced attack. The bottom line is that the act of selling, which is number one in marketing, should not be confused with the act of managing sales.

Sales Staff Management and Development

Once you determine the system and structure your selling plans have been using, you need to define the role of your sales staff. Although some businesses may do away with the sales staff and focus on technology or customer service, most businesses will still employ some form of sales staff. You need to determine how you manage that staff, along with the technology of generating sales.

Depending on the life cycle stage your product is in and the industry you compete in, the role of your sales force will differ. For example, your sales force may have to contend with selling directly to stores and seeking to obtain shelf or floor space, which can entail slotting fees. In this situation, your sales force's role may include negotiating and order taking. They may be required to carry a portable PC unit to record product sales by using bar coding or data entry. In any case, your sales staff will be called upon to perform high- and low-level activities. They must be trained and equipped to perform to the standards required.

You must focus on identifying the best people who represent the best sales methods available. In auditing your sales force development, consider the use of internal versus independent representatives, sales staff size, and recruitment and training of sales staff. Training is usually a major cost consideration. Expenses include training activities, travel, and lodging.

Format 108 provides a method of determining how you will configure your sales force. Select the development activities and tactics that best fit your needs.

Format 108	
Sales Force Tactics	
20___	
By Product	**Sales Force**
ABC	All internal, using 10 knowledgeable professionals located nationally.
ABC2	Mixture of internal and external professionals with solid product knowledge.
By Overall Product Line	Use both internal and external salespeople. Maintain a small yet solid team that knows the product and market.

Internal Sales Promotions

Sales promotions, a subcomponent of promotion, can be separated into two types: external sales promotions, directed at customers as an incentive to buy more, and internal sales promotions, directed at the salesperson as an incentive to sell more. External sales promotion as a marketing mix function will be covered later. In internal sales promotions, you must design an attractive package to motivate your salespeople. While external sales promotions usually consist of value-added incentives, internal sales promotions generally offer cash bonuses or material incentives such as trips. In the consumer package product industry, your sales capacity is dictated by the stores you service; they tell you where and when they will sell your products. Therefore, your sales promotions will often be directed at store chains as well as your sales force.

There are two basic types of internal of sales promotions: bonuses and special incentives. Bonuses are linked to a salesperson's present compensation package, and special incentives are tied to a specific, time-based sales quota. Special incentives are used when trying to move a product quickly. The salesperson's additional compensation can come in the form of cash awards, prizes, and sales premiums.

Use Format 109 to demonstrate what type of internal sales promotions you have been employing.

Format 109	
Internal Sales Promotions	
20___	
By Product	**Sales Promotions**
ABC	*Incentives are based on annual bonuses given for sales over and above a certain level.*
ABC2	*Special awards are given for sales of this particular product.*
By Overall Product Line	*It is our practice to focus on many broad sales promotions to sell product.*

Salesperson Compensation

Most good salespeople are motivated by income, so you need to design a compensation program that fits your financial resources and produces a positive return for a salesperson's efforts. Historically, the consumer package product industry has used low-pressure salespeople because companies in this market depend primarily on stores to sell products, and the salespeople are not directly responsible for the end sale to the customer. Your compensation package must reward a salesperson for service to the store as well as for unit sales. Options include:

- straight commission
- draw against commission (base, payback, rate)
- salary plus commission (base, rate-volume level)
- salary plus commission (base, profit margin level)

Sales figures in Format 110 are based on a single sale (volume of one) of both products.

Sales Territories

Defining where your sales force has been selling is key to productive sales results. Review how you have been assigning salespeople to territories to determine if your assignments have been fair to both you and the salespeople. In the

Format 110

Sales Quota and Compensation Plans

Salesperson	20__ $	Units	20__ $	Units	Rate of Growth (%)	20__ $	Units	Rate of Growth (%)
F. Smith	200,000	10,000	300,000	15,000	50	300,000	15,000	0
J. Doe	400,000	20,000	500,000	25,000	25	500,000	25,000	0
M. Jones	400,000	20,000	400,000	20,000	0	400,000	20,000	0
Total	1,000,000	50,000	1,200,000	60,000	0	1,200,000	60,000	0

Salesperson F. Smith

By Product	Compensation Programs
ABC	2% commission on product sold. Additional 1% bonus if quota is achieved.
ABC2	None
By Overall Product Line	$35,000 salary plus commission.

consumer package product industry you should design your territories using a formula that focuses on time management, customer service, sales, and costs.

Although territories are commonly used, key accounts, especially high-volume customers, need to be included in the equation. In fact, the best method is often to base sales territories on major accounts. Market-based assigning is also beneficial. In this situation, a salesperson represents customer types, based on purchasing habits, competition, or other market-driven forces. The key issue is to review the selection of one or a combination of the three assignment methods to define the most productive selling formula.

Format 111 provides a method of determining how you have been defining your sales territories. Link each product to a salesperson and then establish how that person will service the territories. This may be done by geographic area, based on physical area and customer density, or by key customer accounts.

Format 111

Territory Control Definition   20__

By Product	Territory Assignment	Salesperson Assignment
ABC	Based on key accounts	Based on knowledge of accounts
ABC2	Based on geographic area	Based on knowledge of area
By Overall product line	Mixture of geographic area and key customers	Knowledge is key in majority of sales territories

The tactical aspect of your sales plan may include the components discussed so far or other tactical issues such as:

- sales methods (selling process)

- sales techniques (presentation process)

- sales comparisons—competition

Format 112

Prospecting Methods

20___

By Product	Prospecting Methods
ABC	Salespeople are instructed to push this product at AAA Department Stores.
ABC2	Salespeople are instructed to deal with small stores to obtain shelf space and sell product.
By Overall Product Line	In general, the sales force prioritizes stores that sell more product.

Customer Service and Feedback

Do you have a process in place to monitor customer perceptions, problems, needs, or concerns? You need to make sure you audit your method of tracking customer issues and how well you respond to customers through service. In the old days, customer service was an afterthought or a necessary evil. Today, it is a source of marketing information and opportunities. Service is part of the selling process and is a major element in obtaining and retaining customers. Your audit findings need to address customer service and support and the ability of customers to provide feedback that can be used in creating marketing tactics and actions.

Sales Activity Tracking

The final component of your sales management analysis focuses on how a sale is created. You also need to track and monitor sales results and turn them into actions. This information should be linked to individual salespeople.

Format 113 allows you to track sales activities by individual salespeople, covering the entire sales cycle: approach, interview, demonstration, proposal, and close. The elements to be considered over the last three and the next three years include:

- number of sales calls made per period

- average number of sales calls per sale

- average dollar size per sale and reorder

Format 113	
Sales Activity Tracking	
20___	
By Product	**Sales Activity**
ABC	The normal sales cycle is usually very short (1–2 phone calls in a 1-month period). Salespeople submit a monthly report.
ABC2	Same as above
By Overall Product Line	The sales cycle is short due to knowledge of the customer. Salespeople are expected to make list of contacts and report to management their results.

Marketing Mix Performance—Advertising

Everyone loves the communications side of the marketing plan because it is perceived as glamorous. Although you have more latitude with advertising, it still needs to be structured with clearly defined goals. There are three parts to marketing communications: advertising, promotion, and public relations. If sales is the "push," then communications is the "pull." Advertising transmits your marketing message via several vehicles (media) to your target audience (customers). It allows you to alert your potential customers to your product's benefits and features so they will be motivated to purchase it. In short, advertising enhances and supports your sales and distribution marketing efforts.

In understanding your advertising activities, you need to identify what types of messages you have used and what types of media you should use to communicate with your target audience. When assessing your advertising tactics, keep in mind what type of advertising would best meet your needs: straight, cooperative, or trade. Also consider your objectives (methodology), such as what you have been trying to achieve, whom you have been trying to reach (audience/customer profile), when you have been trying to reach them (time period and one-time vs. campaign series), where you have been trying to contact them (reach and coverage), how often you have been trying to reach them (frequency), and what types of media you have used. You also need to evaluate the creative and production staff who have been preparing your advertising.

The formats in this section provide methods of viewing how you conduct your advertising activities. Complete each format according to the outline and structure shown.

Advertising Budget

As shown in Format 114, the advertising budget should take into account the last three years and the next three years, including creative costs, production costs, media costs, and any cooperative agreement.

Format 114						
Advertising Budget						
Activity	20__ Costs ($)	Percentage of Sales	20__ Costs ($)	Percentage of Sales	20__ Costs ($)	Percentage of Sales
ABC	20,000	1.0	25,000	2.5	25,000	2.5
ABC2	30,000	2.0	25,000	2.5	27,000	2.7
Total	50,000	3.0	50,000	5.0	52,000	5.2

Messages/Themes

The first thing to learn about your advertising is what you are conveying to your audience—the customers. The purpose of this exercise is to determine what message you are projecting.

Format 115 allows you to trace advertising messages and themes used over the last three and the next three years. These messages or campaigns might seek to:

- establish awareness

- inform

- persuade

- remind

- improve attitudes

Creative Developments

Many people consider the creative side of advertising to be glamorous and unfettered, but true marketing management involves establishing parameters for creative people to use in developing advertising. Your objective in this exercise is to establish what types of creative activities you have employed and what limitations you imposed to make the advertising activities conform to your overall marketing approach.

Format 115

Message/Theme for Advertising

20___

By Product	Messages/Themes Used
ABC	*Reinforce product's positives based on age.*
ABC2	*Generate awareness of this new product by informing customers about it.*
By Overall Product Line	*Make customers aware of product features and benefits.*

Format 116 helps you establish key criteria for your creative developments over the last three and the next three years. These include:

- art and design developments

- copy (content) developments

- audio (music) developments

- video/film developments

Format 116

Creative Developments for Advertising

20___

By Product	Creative Developments
ABC	*Primarily using print. Designs with heavy copy have been preferred. Logos and direct response (1-800) are used.*
ABC2	*Focusing on radio and TV. Both audio and video used to interest the viewer.*
By Overall Product Line	*All creative avenues are being used to generate interest and excitement.*

Final Production Management

Once the creative portion of the advertising process has been approved, it must be converted into the actual advertising act. Your objective in this exercise is to establish what activities you use in translating art into action.

Use Format 117 to track your production management decisions over the last three and the next three years with regard to layout and design, photography (stock or custom), typesetting, mechanicals (separations), and printer involvement.

Format 117

Final Production Management for Advertising

20___

By Product	Production Management
ABC	—
ABC2	—
By Overall Product Line	All final production of advertising is handled through outside design firm. AAA Advertising. No problems.

Controlling the Legal Ramifications of Advertising Content

A key issue in business today is how your actions affect the market in which you exist and how you can protect yourself from legal problems. Unfortunately, your marketing acts can have legal ramifications that might hurt your business. Work with an attorney to research the laws, rules, and regulations that could impact your marketing activities. Also record any pending legal actions against your company—lawsuits and violations, for example—plus their predicted outcomes.

Format 118 helps you track legal issues such as:

- claim substantiation

- unfair tactics or deceptive messages

- registered trademark location

- guarantees and testimonials

- use of rereleased images

Format 118

Legal Ramifications of Advertising Content

20___

By Product	Legal Ramifications
ABC	Redesigned labeling to provide better customer warning information.
ABC2	No legal problems
By Overall Product Line	The product is always reviewed by our legal staff as a method of preventing problems.

Media Usage

One fundamental element of advertising is the message; another is the medium used to transmit that message. Medium selection in this context defines where you bought advertising space or time. Media purchasing is the buying of a specific medium's vehicle for message transmission. For example, one medium is print. Within that medium you may have chosen to use *USA Today*, *The Wall Street Journal*, or another daily newspaper.

In this section you will outline your media-buying tactics over the last three and the next three years.

Media factors

- gross rating points (GRP)

- cost per 1,000

- cost per sale

- media demographics (relative to prospects)

- media characteristics (relative to creative requirement)

Format 119	
Media Tactics for Advertising	
20___	
By Product	**Media Tactics**
ABC	*Using GRP, this product is advertised via local TV networks across the United States*
ABC2	*Using cost per sale, this product is advertised in newspapers with coupons tied to a specific store for purchase.*
By Overall Product Line	*Using the method of cost per exposure, all products are advertised in a consistent flow.*

The key is to build your advertising tactics by mixing and matching types of media and media outlets. Your review should pay special attention to what you selected and the reasoning behind those selections.

Media Selection

This section explores which media you use to deliver your advertising message. This will help pinpoint where you are spending your advertising dollars. Previous market research and information on specific media outlets can help you determine which types of media offer you the most efficient and cost-effective way of reaching your audience.

Use Format 120 to evaluate your media selections over the last three and the next three years in local, regional, and national markets. You also should establish evaluation and buying criteria for each medium used.

Exhibit 3-7 provides a list of tactical options from which to select.

Exhibit 3-7

Advertising Audit—Media Options

Medium	Media Outlets
Electronic/Mass marketing	
	TV (broadcast)—spot commercials and tag line on-screen readout
	TV (cable)—spot commercials and tag line on-screen readout
	Radio
	Motion picture insert
	Motion picture (videocassette insert)
Direct marketing/Response (interactive)	
	Direct mail—solo (invitation to inquire and preapproval)
	Direct mail—co-op
	Telemarketing (outbound)
	Telemarketing (1-800-888-900)
	PC/Internet and intranet
	Cable TV
	Direct satellite
	Catalogs and on-line shopping
	Voice mail
	CD-ROM
	CD-ROM on-line services
	Digital video disc and videocassette
	Fax
	Pagers
	Point-of-marketing video connect (in-store kiosks)
Outdoor/General signage	
	Billboard
	Transit
	Window/door signs in stores

continued

Exhibit 3-7 (continued)

Advertising Audit—Media Options

Medium	Media Outlets
	Point-of-purchase displays (floor displays/stands, coupon dispensers, video grocery carts, shelf-talkers/danglers, counter/shelf units, and testers/sampling devices—in-store marketing)
Sports marketing	
	Individual personalities
	Event or sport series
	Teams
	Facilities (e.g., arena)
Print	
	Newspaper
	Freestanding insert
	Brochure/support insert
	Internal imaging (corporate logos, letterhead, envelopes, and business cards)
	Magazine
	Yellow Pages
	Directories
	Event programs
Specialty	
	Posters
	Sales premiums (to customers)
	Slide cards/counter cards
	Shopping bags
	Banners
	Apparel and merchandise
	Prepaid long-distance phone cards
	Digital coupons and checks
	Virtual reality arcade machines
	Flyers and door hangers

Media Selection and Sales Systems

In reviewing how you have been transmitting your message and therefore influencing customers to buy your product, you need to consider how much technology (in terms of automated selling systems) is being used in your overall marketing efforts. If you use new technologies in conjunction with traditional advertising and marketing/sales tactics, your advertising plans need to reflect that. Your marketing mix function (in this case, advertising) will reflect an integration that complements your marketing actions.

Format 120	
Media Selections for Advertising	
20___	
By Product	**Mediums Used**
ABC	Direct mail, cable and broadcast TV, newspapers, and point-of-purchase.
ABC2	Same, plus magazine ads and FSIs.
By Overall Product Line	Using a strong medium and media mix. Concentrate on direct marketing using databases.

Consider the following issues in developing your media selection criteria:

- integration of advertising mix—individual and grouping of media types and specific media outlets

- integration of communication mix—advertising, promotions, and public relations

- integration of marketing mix (all marketing functions)

- integration of other departments

- integration of other companies or divisions (co-op/joint ventures/cross-promotions)

Lead Processing and Management

The lead generation aspect of your advertising program is as important as media selection. The goal with lead management is the same: to alert and prompt a customer to inquire about and purchase the product you are offering. The inquiry aspect is the response to the advertising. This response can be in the form of a customer coming to the place of business and placing an order. The modern world of marketing relies on a physical record of the customer inquiry, known as a *lead*.

Lead processing and management typically appears in your advertising or promotion plans because a lead is normally generated by a communication effort. Even leads that come from sales or other forms of marketing need to be handled as part of your advertising program.

Lead processing and management is the mechanism to produce, record, and direct leads into a structure that categorizes them by product, customer, market, marketing channel or system, sales territory/salesperson, and/or retail location. Leads are tracked by a coding system and monitored for success. The results drive future marketing and lead generation plans. In tracking the effectiveness of your leads, assign a status to each one in the following manner:

- active or inactive

- close/sale or turndown

- referral, unsolicited, or solicited

- customer type (new, current, or former)

The bottom line with leads is their value. This can be measured in many ways, but typically a lead is measured in three ways:

- cost per lead

- cost per response

- cost per sale (from lead)

These three methods will tell you how successful one lead type is compared to another. Of course, lead-to-sale performance is based on many factors, such as a salesperson's willingness to work that lead or a customer's willingness to respond to that lead. The key is to understand how sales and the marketing communication mix produce and work leads. Your audit should target where leads originate, how successful they are, and whether the process needs improvement. Each media mix selected needs to be tied back to a lead.

Again, depending on the level of technology employed in your marketing plans, the lead will play different roles. The introduction of an automated sales system will include lead generation as a centerpiece of marketing performance.

Advertising Response Tracking Results

The final part of a complete advertising audit is checking how effective your advertising activities have been. This analysis is generally part of your ongoing marketing research. Your goal is to assess what tracking activities you have used and what their results were.

Format 121 allows you to track customer recall of your advertising and its effect on purchases over the last three and the next three years.

Marketing Mix Performance—Promotions

Promotion is the second part of the marketing communications equation. Its purpose is to support or enhance your advertising tactics. Promotion takes several forms; in this case, promotion is any marketing event, special value-added program, or the giveaway or sale of secondary products designed to draw attention to your primary products. Sales promotions in this context are unlike sales promotions in sales management, where incentives are set up to encourage salespeople to sell more products. In this environment, sales promotions are established to encourage customers to buy more products. When looking at the

---

Format 121

Advertising Response Tracking Results

20___

By Product	Advertising Response Tracking
ABC	*Tracked media efforts by selected sampling of viewers who watched 70 commercials; was not effective.*
ABC2	*No tracking.*
By Overall Product Line	*As needed, response tracking is employed to establish the effectiveness of our advertising strategies.*

---

ways you have been using promotion, you need to use the same methodology as for advertising; the difference is in the types of media that are available.

Promotion Budget

Format 122 provides a space to establish your budget, including creative costs, production costs, and media costs, as well as any cooperative agreements.

Format 122

Promotion Budget

Activity	20___ Costs ($)	Percentage of Sales	20___ Costs ($)	Percentage of Sales	20___ Costs ($)	Percentage of Sales
ABC	10,000	1.0	12,000	1.2	13,000	1.3
ABC2	8,000	.8	10,000	1.0	12,000	1.2
Total	18,000	1.8	22,000	2.2	25,000	2.5

Assessing Your Message/Theme Tactics

Format 123 helps you assess your promotion messages or themes over the last three years and the next three years. Consider the following promotional goals:

- establish awareness

- inform

- persuade

- remind

- improve attitudes

Format 123

Message/Theme Tactics for Promotion Activities

20___

By Product	Messages/Theme Used
ABC	Taking the advertising theme of reinforcement, this product message was used in trade shows.
ABC2	Same as above, but also utilized couponing and sales promotions.
By Overall Product Line	In general, trade shows and sales incentives reflected the same message used in advertising.

Evaluating Creative Development for Promotion Activities

As with advertising management, your goal is to establish parameters within which creative people can create promotions.

Use Format 124 to evaluate your creative developments over the last three and the next three years. Consider the following developments:

- art and design
- copy (content)
- audio (music)
- video/film

Format 124

Creative Developments for Promotion Activities

20___

By Product	Creative Developments
ABC	Art, audio, and video elements combined with great success for trade show exhibit.
ABC2	Design for coupons including bar codes, was poor. Newer, cleaner sample needs to be created.
By Overall Product Line	All creative developments have used many audio and video elements with great success.

Final Production Management

Once the creative portion of the promotion has been established, it must be converted into the actual promotion. Your objective is to establish what activities you use in translating art into action.

Format 125 will help you assess final production for promotions over the last three and the next three years, including, layout and design, photography (stock or custom), typesetting, mechanicals (separations), and printer involvement.

Format 125	
Final Production Management for Promotion Activities	
20___	
By Product	**Production Management**
ABC	—
ABC2	—
By Overall Product Line	*All final production of promotion materials is handled through our outside design firm—AAA Advertising. No problems.*

Monitoring the Legal Ramifications of Promotion Content

As noted earlier, you should work with an attorney to research the legal ramifications of your promotions. Use this information, plus what you discovered through your market and product audit, to complete this section. Also consider any pending legal actions against your company and their predicted outcomes.

Format 126 provides a place to track the legal issues regarding your promotion activities for the last three and the next three years, including the following actions:

- claim substantiation

- unfair tactics or deceptive messages

- registered trademark location

- guarantees and testimonials

- use of rereleased images

Media Tactics

This section of the audit looks at the methods you use to buy your media. Media buying, especially in the consumer package product and service industries, deals with such things as merchandising and sales promotion.

Format 126	
Legal Ramifications of Promotion Activities	
20___	
By Product	**Legal Ramifications**
ABC	To protect our interests, we need to clearly place our logo on our trade show booth.
ABC2	None
By Overall Product Line	Minor problems only. All promotional activities are reviewed by our legal staff.

Format 127 will help you assess your media strategies over the last three and the next three years, including media demographics relative to prospects, media characteristics relative to creative requirements, media costs, and media availability.

Format 127	
Media Tactics for Promotion Activities	
20___	
By Product	**Media Strategies**
ABC	—
ABC2	—
By Overall Product Line	In summary, promotional media utilizes media characteristics and exposure.

Media Selection

As noted earlier, selecting the proper media or mix of media is the key to effective promotion. In this section you will look at the types of media you use to communicate with your audience. This will help determine where you have committed your promotional dollars and which medium offers the most efficient and cost-effective methods of reaching your customers. Your prior market research can help you obtain this information.

Format 128 provides a place to evaluate your media selections over the last three and the next three years for local, regional, and national markets as well as to establish evaluation and buying criteria.

Refer to Exhibit 3-8 for a list of tactical options.

Exhibit 3-8

Promotion Audit—Media Options

Medium	Media Outlets
Event promotions	
	Time period campaigns
	On-site parties and programs
	Contests/sweepstakes and games
Sales promotions (customer-oriented)	
	Price specials (discounts, rebates)
	Product demonstrations/sampling (in-store/at-home)
	Purchase incentives (in-store couponing, trading stamps, premium offers, money-back offers/cash refunds, value-added purchases/free gifts/bonus packages)
Sponsorship	
	Sports events
	Community and charity projects
	Corporate functions
	Pop music/entertainment tours
	Festivals and fairs
	Arts
Merchandising	
	Endorsements
	Licensing of name
Trade shows	
	Show and booth selection
	Display/exhibit creation
	Show and attendee reception management
	Marketing materials' supply
	Transportation and setup
	Lodging
	Lead generation management

Media Selection and Sales Systems

Promotions need as much consideration as advertising. You need to evaluate how you are managing your marketing mix in transmitting your message and therefore influencing customers to buy your product. Consider what role technology (in terms of automated selling systems) will play in your overall marketing efforts. If you use new technologies in conjunction with traditional

Format 128	
Media Selections for Promotion Activities	
20___	
By Product	**Medium Used**
ABC	*Heavy merchandising, sales promotion (in store), trade shows, and purchase incentives.*
ABC2	*Same*
By Overall Product Line	*Use of a strong mixture of all promotional activities.*

promotion and/or traditional marketing/sales tactics, your promotion efforts need to reflect that.

Consider these issues in developing your media selection criteria:

- integration of promotional mix—individual and grouping of media types and media outlets

- integration of communication mix—advertising, promotions, and public relations

- integration of marketing mix (all marketing functions)

- integration of other departments

- integration of other companies or divisions (co-op/joint ventures/cross-promotions)

Lead Processing and Management

The lead generation aspect of your promotions is as important as your choice of media. The goal with lead management is the same: to alert and prompt a customer to inquire and purchase the product you are offering. The inquiry aspect acts as the response to the advertising. This response can be in the form of a customer coming to the place of business and placing an order. The modern world of marketing relies on a physical record of the customer inquiry, known as a *lead*.

Lead processing and management typically appears in your advertising or promotion plans because a lead is normally generated by a communication effort. Even leads that come from sales or other forms of marketing need to be handled as part of your advertising program.

Lead processing and management is the mechanism to produce, record, and direct leads into a structure that categorizes them by product, customer, market, marketing channel or system, sales territory/salesperson, and/or retail location. Leads are tracked by a coding system and monitored for success. The results drive future marketing and lead-generation plans. In tracking the effectiveness of your leads, assign a status to each one in the following manner:

- active or inactive

- close/sale or turndown

- referral or unsolicited or solicited

- customer type (new, current, or former)

The bottom line with leads is their value. This can be measured in many ways, but typically a lead is measured in three ways:

- cost per lead

- cost per response

- cost per sale (from lead)

These three methods will tell you how successful one lead type is compared to another. Of course lead-to-sale performance is based on many factors, such as a salesperson's willingness to work, that lead or a customer's willingness to respond to that lead. The key is to understand how sales and the marketing communication mix produce and work leads. Your audit should target where leads originate, how successful they are, and whether the process needs improvement. Each media mix selected needs to be tied back to a lead.

Again, depending on the level of technology being employed in your marketing plans, the lead will play different roles. The introduction of an automated sales system will include lead generation as a centerpiece of marketing performance.

Promotions Response Tracking Results

The final part of a complete promotional audit is tracking responses. This task is generally part of your ongoing marketing research function. Use Format 129 to assess the results of your promotion activities and their effect on purchases.

Format 129	
Promotions Response Tracking Results	
20___	
By Product	Promotions Response Tracking
ABC	—
ABC2	—
By Overall Product Line	*No promotional activities conducted.*

Marketing Mix Performance—Public Relations

The final part of the communications side of marketing is public relations. This function interfaces with advertising and promotion. It allows you to take advantage of newsworthy events that could promote your business's image.

In analyzing your past public relations activities, you use the same methodology used in advertising and promotions; the difference comes once again in the medium selection. Pay special attention to your policies concerning media relations, your philosophy on community involvement, and your general publicity practices and public policy.

Budget

Format 130 helps you establish your public relations budget for the last three and the next three years, including creative costs and production costs.

Format 130						
Public Relations Budget						
Activity	**20___ Costs ($)**	**Percentage of Sales**	**20___ Costs ($)**	**Percentage of Sales**	**20___ Costs ($)**	**Percentage of Sales**
ABC	3,000	.3	2,000	.2	1,000	.1
ABC2	4,000	.4	2,000	.2	1,000	.1
Total	7,000	.7	4,000	.4	2,000	.2

Message/Theme Tactics

Format 131 allows you to trace your public relations message or theme strategies over the last three and the next three years. Consider the following goals:

- establish awareness
- inform
- persuade
- remind
- improve attitudes

Format 131

Message/Theme Tactics for Public Relations

20___

By Product	Message/Theme Used
ABC	The message is different than the other section. This message has an attitude awareness to promote positive P.R.
ABC2	Same as above
By Overall Product Line	In summary, the company and all its products have used methods to improve public perception.

Evaluating Creative Development for Public Relations Activities

As with advertising and promotion management, your goal is to establish parameters within which creative people can create public relations activities.

Format 132 will help you evaluate your creative developments over the last three and the next three years. Consider the following developments:

- art and design
- copy (content)
- audio (music)
- video/film

Format 132

Creative Developments for Public Relations

20___

By Product	Creative Developments
ABC	No public relations activities besides press releases.
ABC2	Same as above
By Overall Product Line	Public relations activities have been limited; however, when used, P.R. is effective.

Final Production Management

Once the creative portion of the public relations process has been established, your objective is to establish what activities you use in translating art into action. Format 133 will help you assess final production for public relations campaigns over the last three and the next three years, including, layout and design, photography (stock or custom), typesetting, mechanicals (separations), and printer involvement.

Format 133		
Final Production Management for Public Relations		
20___		
By Product	**Production Management**	
ABC	—	
ABC2	—	
By Overall Product Line	*Final production of all P.R. is handled through our outside design firm, AAA Advertising. No problems.*	

Monitoring the Legal Ramifications of Public Relations

As noted before, you should work with an attorney to research the laws, rules, and regulations you need to be aware of with regard to public relations. Use this information, plus what you discovered through your market and product audits, to complete this section. Also consider any pending legal actions against your company, including lawsuits and violations, plus their predicted outcomes.

Format 134 provides a place to track the legal issues regarding your public relations activities for the last three and the next three years, including:

- claim substantiation

- unfair tactics or deceptive messages

- registered trademark location

- guarantees and testimonials

- use of rereleased images

Format 134	
Legal Ramifications of Public Relations	
20___	
By Product	**Legal Ramifications**
ABC	*None*
ABC2	*None*
By Overall Product Line	*None*

Media Tactics

Your objective in this section is to determine how you select your media. Media selection, especially in the consumer package product and service industries, deals with such things as press releases and media relations.

Format 135 will help you assess your media tactics over the last three and the next three years, including media demographics relative to prospects, media characteristics relative to creative requirements, media costs, and media availability.

Format 135	
Media Tactics for Public Relations	
20___	
By Product	**Media Strategies**
ABC	*Media characteristics*
ABC2	*Same*
By Overall Product Line	*Same*

Media Selection

The proper media mix is the key to public relations effectiveness. In this section you will determine where you have committed your public relations dollars and which medium offers the most efficient and cost-effective methods of reaching your customers. Your prior market research on media usage and media costs can help you obtain this information.

Format 136 provides a place to evaluate your media options over the last three and the next three years for local, regional, and national markets as well as to establish evaluation and selection criteria. Following are suggested media options:

- press releases

- seminars

- open houses/networking parties

- annual reports

- public service announcements

- published articles

- newsletters

- book publishing

Format 136	
Media Selections for Public Relations	
20___	
By Product	**Medium Used**
ABC	*Routine press releases discussing new uses for products.*
ABC2	*Same as above*
By Overall Product Line	*Press releases are the only P.R. activities used.*

Media Relations Practices

This exercise assesses how well you work with the media and how journalists have helped or not helped you in obtaining positive media exposure.

In Format 137 you will assess your media relations practices over the last three and next three years, looking at specific items such as:

- media/press kits

- incentives for favorable coverage (such as premiums)

- timely and accurate communications

Media Selection and Sales Systems

Public relations needs the same consideration you give to advertising and promotions. You need to evaluate how you are managing your marketing mix in transmitting your message and influencing customers to buy your product. You also need to determine what role technology (in terms of automated selling systems) plays in your overall marketing efforts. If you use new technologies in con-

---

Format 137

Media Relations Practices

20___

By Product	Media Relations
ABC	—
ABC2	—
By Overall Product Line	*Relied on personal relationships with contacts in media.* *They have been positive.*

---

junction with traditional public relations or marketing/sales tactics, your public relations plans need to reflect that.

Consider the following issues in developing your media selection criteria:

- integration of public relations mix—individual and grouping of media types and specific media outlets

- integration of communication mix—advertising, promotions, and public relations

- integration of marketing mix (all marketing functions)

- integration of other departments

- integration of other companies or divisions (co-op/joint ventures/cross-promotions)

Lead Processing and Management

The lead-generation aspect of your public relations program is as important as media selection. The goal with lead management is the same: to alert and prompt a customer to purchase the product you are offering. The "inquiry" aspect is the response to the public relations. This response can be in the form of a customer coming to the place of business and placing an order. The modern world of marketing relies on a physical record of the customer inquiry, known as a *lead*.

Lead processing and management typically appears in your advertising or your promotion plans because a lead normally comes from a communication effort. Even leads that come from sales or other forms of marketing need to be handled as part of your public relations program.

Lead processing and management is the mechanism to produce, record, and direct leads into a structure that categorizes them by product, customer, market, marketing channel or system, sales territory/salesperson, and/or by retail location. Leads are tracked by a coding system and monitored for success. The results drive future marketing and lead-generation plans. In tracking the effectiveness of your leads, assign a status to each one in the following manner:

- active or inactive
- close/sale or turndown
- referral or unsolicited or solicited
- customer type (new, current or former)

The bottom line with leads is their value. This can be measured in many ways, but typically a lead is measured in three ways:

- cost per lead
- cost per response
- cost per sale (from lead)

These three methods will tell you how successful one lead type is compared to another. Of course lead-to-sale performance is based on many factors, such as a salesperson's willingness to work that lead or a customer's willingness to respond to that lead. The key is to understand how sales and the marketing communication mix produce and work leads. Your audit should target where leads originate, how successful they are, and whether the process needs improvement. Each media mix selected needs to be tied back to a lead.

Again, depending on the level of technology employed in your marketing plans, the lead will play different roles. The introduction of an automated sales system will include lead generation as a centerpiece of marketing performance.

Community Involvement

Another public relations activity of special importance is getting your name out in the community. You need to devote an allotted amount of time to help local activities grow. Your objective in this exercise is to review your participation in the community and determine if it has had an impact on your product, either directly or indirectly.

Format 138 provides a place for you to evaluate community involvement, such as assisting with charity or arts events, over the last three and next three years.

Public Relations Response Tracking Results

The final step in a complete public relations program is to establish a method of checking the effectiveness of your publicity activities. This task is generally

Format 138

Community Involvement

20___

By Product	Community Involvement
ABC	—
ABC2	—
By Overall Product Line	*Work with all Special Olympics groups in the Midwest.*

a part of your ongoing marketing research function. In this exercise you will assess the effectiveness of your public relations tracking activities.

Use Format 139 to monitor responses to your public relations efforts over the last three and next three years, including their effect on purchases.

Format 139

Public Relations Response Tracking Results

20___

By Product	Response Tracking
ABC	*None*
ABC2	*None*
By Overall Product Line	*None*

Marketing Mix Performance—Legal Issues

Changing Federal Trade Commission laws and other new federal and state rules and regulations can have an impact on your marketing plan. Make sure you are taking the necessary steps to prevent any legal action from being lodged against you. That includes conferring with an attorney. Your main concern is protecting your marketing actions from any legal exposure.

Legal Budget

Format 140 will help you monitor your legal costs over the last three and the next three years.

Format 140

Legal Budget

Activity	20___ Costs ($)	Percentage of Sales	20___ Costs ($)	Percentage of Sales	20___ Costs ($)	Percentage of Sales
ABC	5,000	.5	0	0	3,000	.3
ABC2	2,000	.2	1,000	.1	0	0
Total	7,000	.7	1,000	.1	3,000	.3

Monitoring of Legal Activities

Throughout the communications portion of this marketing audit (advertising, promotions, and public relations) we have discussed the legal ramifications of the processes. In this section you are concerned with marketing-related legal and legislative forces that impact your ability to market products. Your goal is to identify how you monitor and react to these forces.

Format 141 allows you to monitor legal activities over the last three and the next three years, including the following issues:

- product liability law changes and liability insurance costs
- patent/copyright protection
- lobbying/legislative activities
- contract protection

Format 141

Monitoring of Legal Activities

20___

By Product	Monitoring
ABC	Lobbying efforts to prevent federal laws regarding labeling from taking effect.
ABC2	Same
By Overall Product Line	Working with trade associations and private lobbying to monitor all legal activities. So far this has proven successful.

Marketing Implementation Success

Once you determine how you have been marketing your products, you need to see how each function was scheduled in the past. There are two types of schedules to evaluate. One addresses the management of each function's activities (i.e., project manager), and the other addresses media placement schedules. Both types should be evaluated using criteria from the last three and the next three years.

Marketing Activities Timetable

This schedule determines when your marketing projects began and when they ended. Under each function list the events and activities that transpired over the appropriate time period. Format 142 provides a place for you to monitor the timing and progress of your marketing activities.

Media Scheduling and Buying

The placement of your media purchases is very important. How, when, where, who, and what are questions that need to be answered. The following formats are suggested for radio (Format 143), magazines (Format 144), cable and broadcast television (Format 145), outdoor advertising (Format 146), and newspapers (Format 147). Depending on the industry your company is in, these media-buying formats may differ and may be applied in different ways.

Format 142

Marketing Activities Schedule

20___

	Start/Finish (Dates)	On Time (Yes/No)	On Budget (Yes/No)	Comments
Marketing research activities:				
Customer satisfaction	6-01/12-01	Yes	Yes	—
Media tracking	6-01/10-01	Yes	No	Poor projection
Product development activities:				
Pricing activities:				
Distribution activities:				
Sales activities:				
Advertising activities:				
Promotions activities:				
Public relations activities:				
Legal activities:				

Format 143

Radio Purchase Order

Client:

Product: ABC

Message: Reminding customers of special sale

Date Issued: 1-1-2000

Day	Time	Program	Seconds	From/To	Unit Cost	Frequency	Total Cost
M–F	8 a.m.	News	30	Jan.–Feb.	$500	300,000 per day	$1,500
"	12 p.m.	"	"	"	"	"	"
"	5 p.m.	"	"	"	"	"	"

Authorization: S. Carr

Accepted by: M. Beesley

Format 144

Magazine Placement Schedule

Product: | **Begin Date:** | **End Date:** | **Date Approved:** | **Cost:**

Magazine	Jan.	Feb.	March	April	May	June	July	Aug.	Sept.	Oct.	Nov.	Dec.	Total
Name: *ATA Journal*													
Circulation: 30,000													
Closing date: 12-1-2000	1 *1 page*												
Publishing frequency: *monthly*	2 *Reminder*												
Rate: 3 × 5, $995	3 *4-color*												
Number of exposures: 70,000	4 *None*												
Contract time: *1 year*	5 *$995*											$11,940

Product: | **Begin Date:** | **End Date:** | **Date Approved:** | **Cost:**

Magazine	Jan.	Feb.	March	April	May	June	July	Aug.	Sept.	Oct.	Nov.	Dec.	Total
Name:	1												
Circulation:	2												
Closing date:	3												
Publishing frequency:	4												
Rate:	5												
Number of exposures:													
Contract time:													Total:

1: Page
2: Ad type (purpose)
3: Color/B&W
4: Issue/Theme
5: Cost (media placement and/or media placement commissions)

Authorization: *S. Carr*

Accepted by: *M. Beesley*

Format 145

Television Proposal

Product: ABC

Message: Reminding customers of special sale

Date Issued: 1-1-2000

Day	Time	Program	Seconds	Rating	HH (000)	From/To	Unit Cost	Frequency	Total Cost
Fri.	8 p.m.	The Simpsons	30	10.0	500	Jan. only	$5,000	2 million	$20,000

Authorization: S. Carr

Accepted by: M. Beesley

Format 146

Outdoor Proposal

Product: ABC2

Message: Inform customers of improvements

Date Issued: 5-1-2000

Position	Type	Year	Schedule	Unit Cost	No. Times	Total Cost
			Jan. Feb. March April May June July Aug. Sept. Oct. Nov. Dec.			
13th to Main	Billboard	1	x ———— x	$2,000	100,000	$16,000

Authorization: S. Carr

Accepted by: M. Beesley

Format 147

Newspaper Proposal

Newspaper: *Times*

Product: *ABC to ABC2 (product line)*

Message: *Introduction (reinforcement)*

Issued: *1-1-2000*

Day	Type/Day	Ad Size	Gross/Net	Date	Rate	Number of Inserts	Column Inches	Total Cost
M–F	*Morning*	*Full-page*	*$1,500*	*Jan.–March*	*X7*	*1*	*14 × 20*	*$10,500*

Authorization: *S. Carr*

Accepted by: *M. Beesley*

Marketing Budget and Financial Impact Performance

Determining how much it has cost you to market your products and services is a key part of marketing planning. Throughout the marketing planning process, costs and budgets should have been established. The formats in this unit allow you to add these amounts and display the results. They also allow you to check (using percentage of sales) to see if your marketing costs are in line with national averages. This system is not 100 percent foolproof, but it allows you to see if your numbers are realistic and efficient.

In evaluating where your marketing activities stand in terms of cost versus performance, you should assess each marketing function's budget, as well as your combined marketing efforts. Depending on where your products are in the life cycle (determined in your product audit), the cost of marketing will be high or low. The measuring tool used is percentage of sales; you will establish what percentage of a sale is devoted to a marketing expense. For example, if your sales are $100,000 and your cost of advertising is $20,000, your percentage of sales is 20 percent for advertising. The result will determine whether you are spending too much or not enough on your marketing.

Exhibit 3-9 presents guidelines for analyzing sales volume and cost of marketing based on where a product is in its life cycle. As you evaluate your costs versus sales, keep in mind not only the product life cycle, but also whether the costs are accurate and normal (false spending data) and if sales are under or over the norm (poor marketing habits). For example, you may discover that your total marketing expenditures come to an extremely high 60 percent of sales. However, this could be acceptable if your product is in the introduction stage, if the market in which you compete is costly, or if your sales have been low.

It is important to remember that these numbers are just guidelines; depending on your market, your numbers may be proportionately more or less. In the final analysis, marketing costs should be averaged to reflect your overall product line. These cost estimates do not include compensation (e.g., salaries) and operations expenses (e.g., a new MIS investment).

Exhibit 3-9

Marketing Allocation: Product Sales Volume to Cost of Marketing

Product Sales

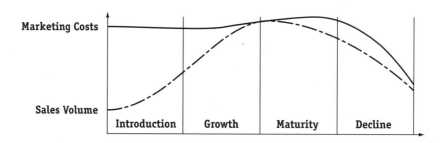

continued

Exhibit 3-9 *(continued)*

Marketing Allocation: Product Sales Volume to Cost of Marketing

	Product Sales Volume			
Sales Activity	Low	High	Steady	Low

Consumer Package Product Industry				
Marketing Activities (percentage of dollars spent on marketing)				
Marketing research and data management	7.5%	3.8%	6.0%	4.5%
Product management and development	5.0%	2.5%	7.5%	3.5%
Pricing	0.0%	0.0%	0.0%	0.0%
Distribution	6.0%	7.0%	8.0%	5.0%
Sales management	10.0%	8.5%	5.0%	3.0%
Advertising	9.0%	5.0%	3.0%	2.0%
Promotions	8.0%	5.0%	3.0%	3.0%
Public relations	2.5%	1.5%	0.5%	0.1%
Legal marketing	5.0%	2.5%	1.0%	1.0%
Total (actual dollars)	53.0%	35.8%	34.0%	22.1%
Range (max.)	45–55%	30–40%	30–40%	15–25%
Total (adjusted dollars)	53.0%	15.0%	10.0%	5.0%

Service Industry				
Marketing Activities (percentage of dollars spent on marketing)				
Marketing research and data management	7.5%	3.8%	6.0%	4.5%
Product management and development	2.5%	1.0%	3.0%	1.5%
Pricing	0.0%	0.0%	0.0%	0.0%
Distribution*	0.0%	0.0%	0.0%	0.0%
Sales management	12.0%	9.0%	6.0%	3.0%
Advertising	9.0%	5.0%	3.0%	3.0%
Promotions	5.0%	2.5%	1.0%	0.5%
Public relations	1.5%	0.5%	0.1%	0.0%
Legal marketing	1.0%	1.0%	1.0%	1.0%
Total (actual dollars)	38..5%	22.8%	20.1%	13.5%
Range (max.)	35–45%	20–30%	15–25%	10–20%
Total (adjusted dollars)	38.5%	12.0%	7.5%	3.5%

*A value of 0.0% is used only if no distrubution, data transfer, or information transmission is expensed.

continued

Exhibit 3-9 *(continued)*

Marketing Allocation: Product Sales Volume to Cost of Marketing

Sales Activity	Product Sales Volume			
	Low	High	Steady	Low

Industrial Manufacturing/Business-to-Business Industry

Marketing Activities (percentage of dollars spent on marketing)				
Marketing research and data management	6.5%	2.8%	4.0%	3.0%
Product management and development	4.0%	2.5%	7.5%	3.5%
Pricing	0.0%	0.0%	0.0%	0.0%
Distribution	8.0%	9.0%	10.0%	6.5%
Sales management	11.0%	9.5%	5.0%	3.0%
Advertising	5.0%	4.0%	3.0%	2.0%
Promotions	2.5%	1.5%	1.5%	0.5%
Public relations	2.5%	1.5%	0.5%	0.0%
Legal marketing	5.0%	2.5%	1.0%	1.0%
Total (actual dollars)	44.5%	33.3%	32.5%	19.5%
Range (max.)	40–50%	30–40%	30–40%	15–25%
Total (adjusted dollars)	44.5%	18.0%	6.0%	2.5%

Totals in this exhibit represent two indicators. Actual dollars are those being spent relative to a constant sales volume. Adjusted dollars are those being spent relative to the real-time sales growth rates.

When evaluating marketing budgets, many people take the percentage of sales literally. In other words, they assume their marketing expenses will fall within these guidelines. This is very dangerous. This exercise gives you a system of checks and balances. The method of evaluating your marketing expenses is to go through each marketing function's budget and then use the percentage of sales process to make sure your numbers are realistic. You may also need to adjust sales totals when comparing individual products versus product line marketing costs.

Expense Reports for Individual Marketing Functions

Format 148 is devoted to listing each function's budget and marketing activity costs. You should be as detailed as possible to make sure you are including all related marketing expenses. This exercise allows you to view your entire marketing function expenses.

Format 148

Individual Marketing Function's Expense Report

Activity	20___ Costs ($)	Percentage of Sales	20___ Costs ($)	Percentage of Sales	20___ Costs ($)	Percentage of Sales
Marketing Research/Data Management						
ABC	10,000	5.0	11,000	6.0	5,000	4.0
ABC2	5,000	3.0	7,000	4.0	10,000	6.0
Total	15,000	8.0	8,000	10.0	15,000	10.0
Product Development						
Total						
Pricing						
Total						
Distribution						
Total						
Sales Management						
Total						
Advertising						
Total						

continued

Format 148 (continued)

Individual Marketing Function's Expense Report

Activity	20___ Costs ($)	Percentage of Sales	20___ Costs ($)	Percentage of Sales	20___ Costs ($)	Percentage of Sales
Promotions						
Total						
Public Relations						
Total						
Legal						
Total						
Total						

Are Your Overall Marketing Activities Expenses on Target?

These statements should include marketing costs only, not related expenses such as compensation for salespeople or distributors. The category of "Other Marketing Expenses" in the next format might include a new MIS system or a database marketing system.

Marketing Function and Product Statement

The following formats look at marketing costs as they relate to your products. This is a good way to identify which products cost you more to market than others.

Now you can perform the same exercise by customer type to see which customer takes the most to reach. You may want to expand on this format by linking marketing costs to sales results and by overall costing to establish customer profitability. Customer type can be defined by the profiles you created through your target market efforts.

Format 149-1

Marketing Function and Product Statement

20___

	Product *ABC*		Product *ABC2*		Overall	
	$	%	$	%	$	%
Marketing Research	10,000	5.0	5,000	3.0	15,000	8.0
Product Development						
Pricing						
Distribution						
Sales						
Advertising						
Promotion						
Public Relations						
Legal						
Total						
Percentage of Sales						

% = Percentage of sales

Marketing Controls Performance

In analyzing your marketing activities, you need to measure the effectiveness of your past and present control procedures. You want to see if the control procedures in place allow you to make adjustments based on changes in the marketplace, because no matter how well planned your marketing tactics are, marketplace variables, new information, and government regulations can force you to alter your course. You also need to evaluate your marketing management tracking systems, which should include checkpoints designed to adjust your marketing thinking.

Monitoring Effectiveness

The primary tools a marketer has available to monitor the marketing plan's performance are sales reports, marketing and media statements, and ongoing marketing audit results. Several of the tracking reports will require you to be knowledgeable in accounting; if you aren't, you need to work with your accountant or controller regarding marketing's role in the financial environment of your business.

Format 149-2

Marketing Function and Customer Targets

20___

	Customer Type		Customer Type		All Customers	
	$	%	$	%	$	%
Marketing Research/ Data Management						
Product Development						
Pricing						
Distribution						
Sales						
Advertising						
Promotions						
Public Relations						
Legal						
Total						
Percentage of Sales						

Format 150

Marketing Plan Reporting and Tracking

20___

Activity	Yes/No	Frequency	Results
Lead Tracking	No	No	None
Sales Reports Tracking	No	No	None
Order Taking/Processing Tracking	Yes	Monthly	Better record-keeping

Reporting and Tracking

Format 150 allows you to assess your monitoring activities over the last three years and the next three years.

Format 151						

Marketing Activity Tracking by Income Statement Analysis

	20___		20___		20___	
Item:	$	Percentage	$	Percentage	$	Percentage
Gross sales						
Product A:* ABC	600,000	—	700,000	—	600,000	—
Product B:* ABC	100,000	—	200,000	—	400,000	—
Total*						
Less returns/allowances						
Net sales	700,000	—	900,000	—	1,000,000	—
Cost of goods sold						
Beginning inventory						
Cost of goods purchased						
Total merchandise handled						
Ending inventory						
Total						
Gross profit*						
Gross profit margin*						
Marketing expenses						
Sales compensation						
Marketing functions*	100,000	14	150,000	17	300,000	30
Shipping	80,000	10	120,000	15	200,000	10
Payroll taxes and insurance						
Regional office expense						
Total						
General administrative expenses						
Executive salaries						
Clerical expense						
Payroll taxes and insurance						
Office expenses						
Depreciation						
Credit/collections						
Research/development costs						
Other expenses						
Total						
Total expenses						
Net profit						

*Numbers are produced by marketing management.

Note: Percentage represents percent of sales as it relates to costs.

Marketing Activity Tracking by Income Statement Analysis

Format 151 allows you to see how your marketing actions have impacted your overall financial health. You are provided an income statement that will need to be prepared with the help of your controller or accountant.

Industry-specific income statements are critical in this exercise. Although the role of marketing in terms of costing and its relationship to product/income source sales is basically the same, the environment in which it is interpreted can vary. For example, the cost of goods section may be called cost of materials or named specifically for a particular industry (i.e., cost of funds—financial world). The items that fall under this section may vary as well.

Updating

As you track and monitor your marketing management performance, you need to be able to intercept your marketing tactics so that you can adjust your plan, alter tactics, and prepare for next year's marketing plan. Format 152 provides a place to map out secondary plans if they become needed.

Marketing research adjustments

- changes to marketing plan (strategies, projections, costs, etc.)

- new plan of action

Contingency planning

- alternative tactics

- benchmarks for safety valve

Format 152			
Contingency Planning			
20___			
Activity	**Yes/No**	**Frequency**	**Results**
Marketing Research Adjustments	*No*	—	—
Contingency Planning	*Yes*	*Quarterly*	*Adjust to customer attitudes/wants.*

Unit 4

Preparing for the Analysis and Planning Phases

You have just completed a full marketing management audit by isolating and reviewing the three elements of marketing: market, product, and marketing actions. Now that you have gone through the audit, asked the tough questions, and compiled a mountain of data, how do you go from research to analysis to planning? The answer is in this section, which is a bridge between this book and the next book in this series: *Developing Successful Marketing Strategies*.

This book provides a structure in which to load your audited data to define and identify needs, problems, and opportunities. Although your findings will present you with obvious issues for resolution, you need a certain amount of preparation before you move to this next stage. You need to organize your data in a manner that can be easily translated into strategies, tactics, and actions.

Organizing the Audit Data

The first step in converting your data into an analysis (drawing conclusions) is to refine the data. This is accomplished by arranging the data in a way that highlights data relationships. Look at the raw data captured in your audit and pick out key data points.

Building Your Data Pool

Your audit data (input data) must be clean, clear, and defined by the three elements of the audit:

- identification of the marketplace and the customers

- value assessment of the products

- evaluation of the effectiveness of your marketing

Once you finalize your pool of raw data, you need to list key areas of concern or attractiveness. Identify these areas by name and then explain the reasons for your observations. In other words, you need to locate measurement points that stand out more than others.

Preparing for the Analysis

In readying yourself for the analysis stage, you need to supplement the raw audit data with a summary tool. This entails building some type of matrix or perceptual map that shows (at a glance) key data points referenced to other key data points that intersect with either resulting calculated data or a statement of status.

Exhibit 4-1 presents a structure that allows you to isolate all the marketing elements that drive your business. It is a model one might invent to compile and arrange the following elements:

- markets (segment profiles and status)

- customers (statistical, status, and business specific profiles)

- products (status)

- marketing actions (N/P/O: needs, problems and/or opportunities)

This example frames these various marketing elements to show your findings at a glance and to prepare you to expand upon what your audits have uncovered. The example displays your audit results in a narrative form, but you can in many cases insert quantitative numbers to measure performance.

Once this is accomplished, you can begin looking at the early returns that will form your conclusions. The objective is to craft your data in a fashion that does not alter the objective findings, but also to shape the data to help you locate marketing issues. You may want to use statistical marketing tools, but you need to arrange the data in a manner that allows you to extract the information you need.

Demand Assessment

A key objective of your research, analysis, and planning is to establish the degree of demand. This information will enable you to better state your inten-

Exhibit 4-1

Analysis Preparation

Market	Customer	Market Status	Customer Profile — Statistical	Customer Profile — Status	Customer Profile — Business Specific	Product Status	Research/ Data Mgmt	Product Mgmt/Dev	Pricing	Distribution	Sales Mgmt	Advertising	Promotions	Public Relations	Legal Mktg
Market: A	Customer: 1	New	X***	New	X**	Current	N/P/O	N/P/O	N/P/O	N/P/O	N/P/O	N/P/O	N/P/O	N/P/O	N/P/O
	2	New	X***	Former	X**	Current	N/P/O	N/P/O	N/P/O	N/P/O	N/P/O	N/P/O	N/P/O	N/P/O	N/P/O
	3	Current	X***	New	X**	Former	N/P/O	N/P/O	N/P/O	N/P/O	N/P/O	N/P/O	N/P/O	N/P/O	N/P/O
B	1	Former	X***	Current	X**	Current	N/P/O	N/P/O	N/P/O	N/P/O	N/P/O	N/P/O	N/P/O	N/P/O	N/P/O
C	1	New	X***	New	X**	New	N/P/O	N/P/O	N/P/O	N/P/O	N/P/O	N/P/O	N/P/O	N/P/O	N/P/O
	2	Current	X***	Current	X**	Former	N/P/O	N/P/O	N/P/O	N/P/O	N/P/O	N/P/O	N/P/O	N/P/O	N/P/O
Overall		Mixture	X***	Mixture	X**	Mixture	N/P/O	N/P/O	N/P/O	N/P/O	N/P/O	N/P/O	N/P/O	N/P/O	N/P/O
Market: A	Customer: 1	New	X***	New	X**	Current	N/P/O	N/P/O	N/P/O	N/P/O	N/P/O	N/P/O	N/P/O	N/P/O	N/P/O
	2	Former	X***	Former	X**	Current	N/P/O	N/P/O	N/P/O	N/P/O	N/P/O	N/P/O	N/P/O	N/P/O	N/P/O
	3	Current	X***	New	X**	Former	N/P/O	N/P/O	N/P/O	N/P/O	N/P/O	N/P/O	N/P/O	N/P/O	N/P/O
B	1	Current	X***	Current	X**	Current	N/P/O	N/P/O	N/P/O	N/P/O	N/P/O	N/P/O	N/P/O	N/P/O	N/P/O
	2	New	X***	New	X**	New	N/P/O	N/P/O	N/P/O	N/P/O	N/P/O	N/P/O	N/P/O	N/P/O	N/P/O
C	1	New	X***	Current	X**	Former	N/P/O	N/P/O	N/P/O	N/P/O	N/P/O	N/P/O	N/P/O	N/P/O	N/P/O
Overall		Mixture	X***	Mixture	X**	Mixture	N/P/O	N/P/O	N/P/O	N/P/O	N/P/O	N/P/O	N/P/O	N/P/O	N/P/O

Market Status	Statistical	Status	Business-Specific*	Status
New	Demographics	New	Life-Cycle	New
Current	Socio-economics	Current	Product Usage	Current
Former	Product Usage	Former	Customer Profitability	Former
	Lifestyle		Customer Risk	
	Psychographic			
	Shopping Habits			
	Media Usage			

N/P/O: Needs, problems, and/or opportunities that exist in this intersection.

In addition to N/P/O, you can enter sales, costs, strategy, tactics, actions, performances, and other key indicators.

*Because each market is different, the Business-Specific Profiles are shown as examples.

** Because of limited space, an "X" has been placed to reflect a selected description.

Market, Customer, and Product types are mixed and matched to display examples.

tions regarding goals, budgets, and actions. Knowing your level of demand, is a data point on its own that can drive the next step in the process.

To understand demand, you need to know how many products are being sold, how often, at what price, in what period of time, and under what conditions. You'll need to know the cost versus return of capturing and keeping a customer.

Providing Support Materials

With every document you prepare, you need to include only the pertinent information. If you include every single piece of data, your document would be difficult to read and understand. Prepare a section of support materials for readers to consult for further verification of your marketing decisions.

Preparing the Exhibit Section

Developing the support material section begins with collecting and organizing your sources of information, organizing the contacts you made in collecting that information, and describing how the results of the information were produced. Then you need to make available examples of the data you obtained, such as actual research reports. Finally, you will provide the methodologies you used in producing the data estimates. Your objective is to compile all of the following information:

- information source, including each contact's name, address, and phone number

- information (results) obtained

- examples (actual raw data)

- methodologies used, including processes, models, or formulas

Preparing for Strategic and Tactical Marketing Plans

The ultimate goal of the audit is to collect data that can be analyzed to the extent where conclusions can be formed and recommendations can be offered. In other words, after the analysis you need to identify the efforts you will undertake to deliver the results or changes desired. Therefore, the plan for action must be built from the audit and the analysis.

The marketing plan comes in two forms: strategic (one to two years) and tactical (annual). After completing this book and the next book in the series, which addresses the analysis and strategic marketing plan, you're ready for the marketing plan (*Preparing the Marketing Plan*). That's where the rubber meets the road. Audits, analyses, and strategic plans are all designed to get to actions. Therefore, the final element in closing out your auditing efforts and preparing to move to the next level centers on the planning aspect.

Strategic Marketing Plan

Once the analysis is complete, you need to translate your thoughts into direction. Although in many cases you can move directly to the annual marketing plan, to understand how all the marketing pieces fit together, we will discuss the strategic marketing plan relationship first.

The strategic marketing plan takes the conclusions and recommendations formulated in the analysis and converts them into the mission statement, goals, objectives, and strategies. These elements form the overall structure that will drive your business for the next one to two years. The main focus is the strategies, for they establish how you will respond to the market, customer, product, and marketing issues your company faces. Therefore, you need to organize your audited data to form your strategic direction. You need to view your data not only as responses or findings, but as indicators that can be translated into actions.

The Marketing Plan

The marketing plan is the final destination for one's marketing thoughts. It uses the analyzed data from the audit and the resulting strategic direction to map out a plan of action for one business year. This tool becomes the working document to carry out your marketing activities such as advertising, sales, distribution, and pricing. Exhibit 4-2 demonstrates how the data contained in the audit link the analysis and marketing planning stages.

The marketing audit is a tool that can provide insight into current and future problems, needs, and opportunities regarding your markets, customers, products, and marketing efforts. The secret is to organize your thoughts through the processes and formats provided here, as well as your own ideas. With accurate, time-sensitive data you can build a strong, consistent, and results-oriented marketing effort.

Exhibit 4-2

Process Flow—Audit to Plan

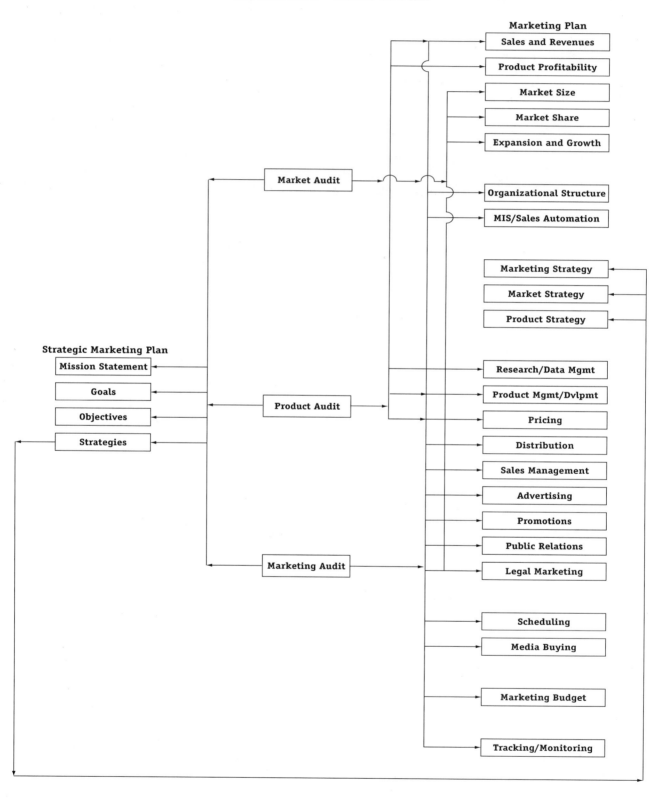

About the Author

David Parmerlee is a senior manager in marketing and product development with USA Group. He worked for Banc One Financial Services for four and a half years, directing its marketing product management and development efforts.

In his more that ten years as a marketing consultant he helped many types and sizes of businesses sort through the mystery of true marketing management by providing them with solid marketing strategies and tactics. These strategies and tactics came from his experiences with processes he developed for marketing research, analysis, and planning. The processes were designed to produce consistent, stable growth, low risk, and solid results. His books are based on these processes.

Mr. Parmerlee's books and processes are simple but comprehensive. They provide structure and substance to marketing management, and they elevate marketers to a level equal to accounting, finance, and production managers. His books, available in three languages, have been read by thousands of business leaders, students, educators, entrepreneurs, and marketers all over the world. Managers and journalists have hailed his marketing planning book as one of the best in the industry.

Mr. Parmerlee's goal is and will always be to share information on how to apply real world and practical marketing, using solid processes to produce secure and consistent marketing results.

The American Marketing Association is the world's largest and most comprehensive professional association of marketers. With over 45,000 members, the AMA has more than 500 chapters throughout North America. The AMA sponsors 25 major conferences per year, covering topics ranging from the latest trends in customer satisfaction measurement to business-to-business and service marketing, attitude research and sales promotion, and publishes nine major marketing publications.

For further information on the American Marketing Association call toll free at 800-AMA-1150.

Or write to:

The American Marketing Association
311 South Wacker Drive
Suite 5800
Chicago, IL 60606-2266
Fax: 800-950-0872
URL: http://www.ama.org